WICCA UNVEILED

THE COMPLETE RITUALS OF MODERN WITCHCRAFT

BY

J. PHILIP RHODES

5 HIGH STREET
GLASTONBURY
SOMERSET BA6 9DP
TEL/FAX: 01458 835974

Layout and typesetting by Wes Freeman
Cover art and all illustrations © Trystan Mitchell 1999
Printed and bound in Great Britain by Redwood Books

ISBN 0 9536745 0 9

To my wife, who always wanted to know.

To all those who in some way influenced the outcome of this book.

Also to Nigel and Seldiy, who first introduced me to Wicca.

"In perfect love and perfect trust."

CONTENTS

FOREWORD

The Craft of Wicca is not the achievement of one person, it is created through the work of many hands. The rituals of Wicca are not set in stone and they allow for the individual to build their own character into the rites. This is why some covens prefer to do things differently to others. Wicca is an evolving system and it will continue to evolve as others add to it. The rituals of Wicca are worked alone or as a group.

I would like to thank all those who have helped to make Wicca what it is today: Gerald Gardner, Doreen Valiente, Arnold and Patricia Crowther, Alex and Maxine Sanders, Janet and Stewart Farrar, and all those whom I have forgotten to name.

Although the practicing of witchcraft is no longer a capital offence in Britain, the persecution of witches continues. People are no longer afraid of witches, but they still mistrust and avoid them. Because of this, most Wiccans continue to hold their rites in secret, and this secrecy allows the myths and half-truths about the practices of paganism to proliferate. The only way forward is to remove the veil that surrounds modern witchcraft. Only when witchcraft becomes fully understood can it become socially acceptable.

Over the years there have been many articles written about Wicca and witchcraft. Some of these are genuine and some are not. Many of the rituals have been disclosed but only partially or inaccurately. Until now, the only way to learn witchcraft was to join a coven and be taught by word of mouth. This is the traditional way in which Wicca is taught and the way in which I myself learnt.

This book is the culmination of many years practicing the art of Wicca. Its purpose is to lift the veil that surrounds Wicca so that it may be better understood. In this book can be found the complete rituals of Wicca laid down as a step-by-step guide and explained in a way that can be clearly understood by both the experienced and the inexperienced.

Blessed be.

John Philip Rhodes

CHAPTER ONE

THE CRAFT OF WICCA

The Craft of Wicca was developed by Gerald Gardner and introduced to the British public during the 1950s. Using material gathered from a New Forest coven and the Order of the Temple Orientis, Gardner produced a magical synthesis which allowed traditional witchcraft to engage with the modern world. In the years that followed, Alex Sanders rewrote many of the Gardnerian rituals and established his own coven. Though some covens still identify themselves as "Gardnerian" or "Alexandrian", the old divisions seem less important today, and the ritual system elucidated here draws on both traditions.

Wicca is founded upon the fertility of the land and the continuation of life. In Wicca, all living things are sacred. In nature, both masculine and feminine play equally important roles. The essence of all that is masculine is portrayed as the Horned God and the White Goddess portrays the essence of all that is feminine. There are no hard and fast rules in Wicca other than: "Do as thou wilt - but harm thou none!"

There are three sacraments in Wicca: Love, Life and Truth. These are valued above all else; without them there can be no harmony within the group. In our society, honesty, compassion and respect for life are rare. This is one of the reasons why many people are attracted to Wicca as a way of life. Although many pagans call themselves Wiccans, a true Wiccan is someone who has been initiated into the Craft.

The rituals of Wicca are designed to develop an awareness and an understanding of the unseen energies that surround us. Everything that exists is shaped by the same Creator and joined together by the strands of a vast cosmic web. Therefore there is no part of us that is not "of the Gods". Through the rituals of Wicca, we may once more connect with Mother Earth and restore the harmony between us.

Wiccans and pagans will strive to protect Mother Earth and the creatures that live upon Her; they will also try to ensure the continuation of the fertility of the land. The ultimate aim of both Wiccans and pagans is to live in harmony with man and nature. Wiccans embrace the Buddhist belief that all life is both sacred and cyclic. All things are reborn after death, albeit in a different shape or form. Wiccans will not harm any living creature deliberately, nor will they attempt to use their magic for personal gain. Wiccans are classed as 'white' or good witches and will, upon request, perform healing rituals for the sick and cast spells for the advancement of others, but they should never ask for a reward of any kind.

The rules of conduct by which Wiccans abide forbid the harming and the restricting of others unless in self-defence. Wiccans are trained in the arts of spellcasting, healing, astrology and divination. They are also sometimes able to end periods of stagnation by encouraging favourable conditions to occur and allowing a window of opportunity to open.

Evil or "black witches" as they are sometimes called, differ greatly from Wiccans. A black witch will attempt to force an event to occur that will further their own standing, and cares little for any repercussions this may have upon the natural patterns of destiny or the harm it may do to other people.

Gerald Gardner, who is hailed as the father of Wicca, states that the word Wiccan originates from the Saxon word Witoan, which means Wise One. Doreen Valiente, who also took a large part in the creation of Wicca, states that the word Wiccan comes from the Germanic word Witgan, which also has the same meaning. Gerald Massey in his Book of the Beginnings states that the word Wicca stems from the Egyptian word Huka or Heka, which means magic. A practitioner of Huka is called a Hukan or Hekan. - One who follows the Goddess Hecate. The word witchcraft is believed to stem from the word Witcraft, which means The Craft of the Wise. Wicca is referred to as The Craft by Wiccans and those who practice Wicca are considered to be Of the Craft. The Craft of Wicca is also thought to mean the art of weaving spells.

THE PASSWORD

In the craft of Wicca there is a secret password, *"In perfect love and perfect trust."* When this password is given from one Wiccan to another, it must mean what it says - that there must be perfect love and perfect trust between all the members of the craft. Only through this can a harmonious balance be struck within a coven. All Wiccans must abide by this law.

THE GREETING

When Wiccans meet others whom they suspect of being witches, they never ask them directly if they are witches. Wiccans tactfully inquire, "Are you of the craft?" If an affirmative answer is received, a fencing game usually follows where each participant discovers the others affiliations. When Wiccans meet, they give the greeting, "Blessed be!" or "Merry meet". When Wiccans part company, they say "Blessed be!" or "Merry meet, merry part, merry meet again!" When a witch greets another witch of a different sex, the greeting is always given with a kiss.

THE BOOK OF SHADOWS

In the craft of Wicca, it is traditional to keep a magical record. This magical record is called The Book of Shadows and has been kept by witches since time immemorial. The Book of Shadows is written in the witch's own hand-writing - this practice stems from the burning times, when to keep such a book was forbidden and any handwriting within it was incriminating evidence. The Book of Shadows is a record of all the knowledge that a witch acquires during training and is kept hidden from outsiders.

THE MEASURE

Witches have existed among us for over five thousand years but it was not until the Middle Ages that the fear of witches led to their persecution. During the Civil War, persecution reached a crescendo and witches went to great lengths to prevent their disclosure. To ensure against betrayal, a length of cord was used to record the height, chest, hips, and head and foot size of each member of the coven, known as: "The Measure". In the event of disclosure, the measurements could be used to implicate the betrayer to the authorities. A measure was believed to contain part of the soul and could be used magically against the betrayer.

COVENS

Not all witches work in covens. Many witches choose to work alone, either because they do not have a coven nearby, or simply because they are more comfortable working in solitude. At one time, it would have been very difficult to find a coven, let alone gain entry to one. However, the vigilance of covens is now relaxing, and those that request entry into the craft are usually invited to a social gathering to meet others in the coven, where their ability to work as part of a group is assessed.

In the absence of the candidate, the group discusses the matter. If no one has any misgivings the candidate is invited to return as a guest to attend a working circle. The candidate is allowed to work with the group for three months. After this time, if the group deems them suitable, they must either take the oath and take the first-degree initiation or they must leave the group. The tradition of taking the measure is still used to ensure that they keep their oath. Some covens retain this measure and some return it to the owner.

COVEN MEETINGS

In Wicca, seasonal celebrations are held eight times a year on the Sabbats. Meetings are also held upon the nights of the full moon - the full moon meetings are called Estbats. The full moon meetings are held to worship the Goddess of the Moon. Training nights are also held for initiates on a regular basis. These nights are decided upon by the Priest and Priestess. Each member of the coven that attends a meeting must bring with them a bottle of wine or some food. Some covens ask for small donations of cash (whatever can be spared) toward the upkeep of the temple - this is to pay for candles, incense and the like. Upon the Sabbats, coven members that are available must help with the preparations for the celebration. Each member that is attending a ritual must be there before the appointed hour, those that are not are barred entry until the circle is over. Those that attend meetings give an agreed number of knocks on the door to gain entry. Upon gaining entry, they then give the password.

CHAPTER TWO

THE WITCH'S TOOLS

In any ritual, it is important that all the equipment is thoroughly cleansed, purified and charged, before use.

THE CEREMONIAL DAGGERS

In the Craft of Wicca, there are two ceremonial daggers, the purist knife and the athame. The purist knife is a utility knife that has a white handle and a single, sharp cutting edge. The white-handled knife is used mostly for cutting. The athame (pronounced athamay) has a black handle and a blunt, tapered, double-edged blade. The black-handled athame is used for the conjuration of the circle and for commanding the spirits. According to pagan lore, the spirits are afraid of steel and this is why iron is rarely found in ancient temples. Both of these tools are often inscribed with symbols of power. It is also the tradition to personalise tools by writing your name on them in runic or Sanskrit. The daggers and their magical symbols can be found in the Key of Solomon.

An athame must never be allowed to touch the ground, as it will discharge itself into the earth. No-one but the owner should ever touch the Athame, the Tarot cards, or any personal jewellery. It is the belief that all personal items become attuned to their owner. To charge a new athame with magical power, the blade, duly cleansed and consecrated, must be placed upon the blade of an athame that has already been charged. If this is not possible, then the athame may be placed upon a charged pentacle (a pentacle that has had power already beaten into it) and charged in that manner. Always clean the athame blade after the ceremony of the cakes and wine. Never put the blade of the athame into salt water, as this will rust the blade very quickly. I personally do not insert my athame into the wine; I use the phallic wand.

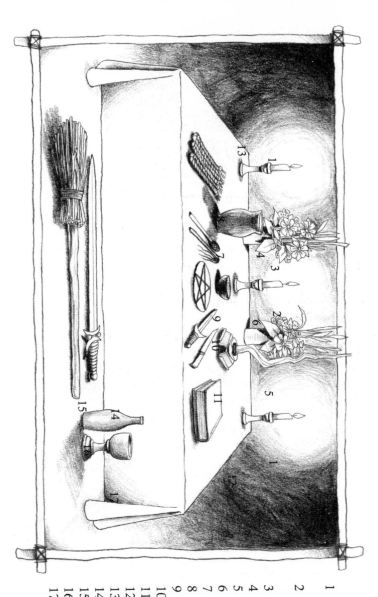

1   Altar candles
     (green left, red right)
2   Central candle
     (silver, white or gold)
3   Flowers
4   Water
5   Incense
6   Salt dish
7   Scourge
8   Solar wand
9   Pentacle
10   Athame
11   White-handled knife
12   Instruction book
13   Cords & other materials
14   Sword of power
15   Broom
16   Wine
17   Chalice

THE SWORD OF POWER

In Wicca, a sword is often used instead of an athame for the casting of the circle. The sword is an extension of the athame and obtains its name from the time when only those who were 'entitled' (those with titles. i.e., coats of arms) were allowed to carry swords. In later times the sword became a symbol of the powerful. The Lords of the land were responsible for those who worked their land and they understood the nature of the pagan rites. Lords often attended the meetings anonymously and they presided over matters of judgment (hence the term, judged by the sword). During the burning times, the land owner would become an anonymous figure known only as the Magister and he would disguise himself as the Horned God. Through this, the sword became a symbol of judgment and power. A sword of power is usually only used by the Priest and it is usually drawn in matters of judgment. The use of the sword in casting the circle originates from The Key of Solomon.

INCENSES AND PERFUMES

Incense is regarded as the purifying element of air, and it is employed in every temple to cleanse the place of worship and the things contained within it. In Wicca, incense is used for many purposes. There are incenses that are used for purification, incenses for attracting certain qualities, and incenses used to create atmospherics. The incense used in the planetary rituals must correspond exactly to the rite (see the table of correspondences).

When burned in large quantities - and especially when mixed with Dittany of Crete - incense gives off a lot of smoke. This dims the surroundings and creates a timeless feeling. In magic, smells are important. They can help the mind to create images of times past, and Gods long dead. This is why perfumes and incenses that are to be used in ritual magic should bring to mind the image required. For example, an image of a rose is easy to see in the mind. However, by using a rose scent, the image can be brought nearer to life. Incense can be purchased in many forms but most Wiccans buy loose incenses and gums, which they blend to ancient recipes.

MAKING AN INCENSE BURNER.

An incense burner is often called a censer or a thurible. Thuribles can be purchased in many forms, ranging from minute brass objects designed to hold sticks and cones, to swing censers. Of these, swing censers are the most expensive and are only available from church suppliers. A cheap thurible for burning loose incenses however, can be made quite cheaply from a bowl with one to two inches of sand in the bottom (this stops the bowl from becoming too hot to hold). All that is needed then is a packet of charcoal discs, and some loose incense. To burn the incense, just light a charcoal disc, and wait until it has heated through, then put a spoonful of the incense on it.

THE SCOURGE

The scourge, or flail, is a small instrument that is used in many religions for the purpose of spiritual cleansing. In Wicca the scourge is used to purify, to beat power into the pentacle, and uphold discipline within the coven. The Wiccan scourge is constructed from nine lengths of cord, or soft leather strips, of 9 inches, each strip having nine knots tied into it.

MAGICAL WANDS

There are two principal wands used in the craft of Wicca, the Phallic or Solar wand and the Caduceus. The solar or phallic wand is a symbol of the creative power of the Horned God and it can be found in two forms. Either as a rod carved into the shape of a phallus, or as a straight shaft of wood with a pinecone mounted on it - this is adorned with red and green ribbons. The phallic or solar wand is believed to bestow the gifts of health and fertility upon those who touch it - as is the Maypole.

The Caduceus is the wand of Hermes and is regarded as having the power to impart his healing powers. A caduceus can be constructed from a straight length of dowelling that is topped with two clay wings. Two snakes, one black, one white, are then woven together up the length of the rod (crossing over three times) to end facing toward each other at the top (wire can be used to form the snakes, which can then be covered with clay and baked hard).

MAGICAL SYMBOLS

Magical symbols may be inscribed upon any ritual item in the Craft of Wicca. These magical symbols are called sigils. Each planet has its own particular glyph, sigil, number, and geometric figure that represents its power. The most powerful of these symbols are the pentagram and the hexagram. According to the Key of Solomon, these symbols protect the wearer against evil spirits and also endow the conjurer with the power to command any spirits that appear unto him when the symbols are shown. In the Key of Solomon, the Hexagram is drawn upon a piece of parchment and is worn upon the hem of the robe. The pentagram is drawn upon a disc and then shown to the spirit upon its appearance. The Greek philosopher Pythagoras first conceived the practice of creating sigils from planetary squares and the use of geometrical figures in magic.

THE PENTACLE

A pentacle is a round flat copper or brass disc, six-inches or more in diameter, that has a pentagram inscribed upon it. Small items that are to be charged can be placed upon a pentacle that has had energy 'beaten into it'. The item then draws its power from the pentacle. To charge a pentacle, it is first placed in the centre of the circle, then beaten by the coven who each take turns 'beating in the power' by striking the disc with the flat of their hand. In this manner, the thought and the energy that are held in the mind are directed into the pentacle, charging it with energy. Once sufficient energy has been beaten into the pentacle it is then placed on the altar and the item to be charged is placed upon it. The scourge can also be used for this purpose.

THE CHALICE AND THE CAULDRON

The cauldron is the symbol of the womb of the Great Mother, depicted as the cauldron of Cerridwen. The cauldron is a symbol of protection, nourishment and wisdom. The chalice is a smaller representation of the cauldron.

THE CORDS

In the Craft of Wicca, the passing of a wish (otherwise known as a spell) is often accomplished with the use of a magical cord or thread. This stems from a very old pagan practice of tying knots in a piece of thread. The cord or thread represents the span of a man's life, which is already predetermined at birth by fate. The tying of a knot in the measure of a person was believed to have varying effects upon the victim's life. In the Wiccan art of tying knot spells, thick cords of varying colours are used. Every colour used in cord magic has a special meaning, as do the colours of the candles used in candle magic.

In Wicca there are three main cords that are used above all others, although the colour of a cord worn by an individual varies according to their taste. A red cord represents life and it symbolizes an umbilical cord. A white cord represents purity and the powers of light. A black cord represents evil and the powers of darkness.

CHARMS, AMULETS AND TALISMANS

Charms bring good favour to the wearer, amulets protect the wearer against evil, and talismans draw power to the wearer. All of them protect in their own manner. Charms, amulets and talismans can be constructed from any organic material.

To make a charm, talisman or amulet, you must first know what materials are fit for the purpose for which the item is intended. Go to the table of correspondences and locate the aspect that you wish to call upon. Study the list of colours and materials that correspond to the power you require. Any of those materials listed under that heading can be used for your charm. Choose what you can obtain most easily from the index. For example, if you wish to construct a love charm, you can make one from a blank copper disk and engrave it with the sigils of the spirits that you wish to call upon. Alternatively you can draw a charm in ink upon paper. You can also write your wish on paper and burn it. Perform the construction of the item upon the correct day and hour given for the rite, and inscribe your wish upon the material, whether it is as a magical number, an anagram, a sigil, or a magical script. If paper is to be used, then coloured paper that corresponds to the rite can be used. The charm must then be purified through the elements. The charm is then charged with the athame. To charge an item it must be placed upon the charged pentacle and bathed in an imaginary blue light. The pentagram must then be drawn over the charm using the athame with the words of consecration. Energy is then directed into the item using the athame. The charm is then ready to serve its new purpose.

MAGICAL NUMBERS

Magical numbers are often used to represent names; the numerical value of a letter is worked out in the following way:

A	B	C	D	E	F	G	H	I
J	K	L	M	N	O	P	Q	R
S	T	U	V	W	X	Y	Z	
1	2	3	4	5	6	7	8	9

Example 1:
Lynn becomes 3755 add together 3+7 and 5+5, this gives 10 and 10. Add these together, and you get 1+1 = 2. Two then, is the number of Lynn, and would be used upon a charm to represent her name.

In Numerology, each number represents a different aspect of character, i.e.:

1. Drive, ambition.

2. The feminine

3. Talent, luck, gaiety, versatility, introversion

4. Melancholy, practicality

5. Restlessness, instability, sexual drives

6. Harmony, love, domesticity

7. Mysticism, spirituality

8. Success, power, wealth, extroversion

9. Malefic number

Example 2:
Marilyn Monroe = 419375 435965 = 29 + 32. 29+32 =61. 6+1 =7.
Marilyn's number is seven.

THE BESOM

The witch's broom is called a besom. The besom is made at Imbolc from birch twigs. One end of the handle is carved into the shape of a phallus and inserted into a bundle of broom or birch twigs. The twigs must then be secured to the shaft. The Besom represents the conjoining of male with female, the handle is the phallus, and the twigs are the brush. A Besom is believed to have the power to span the worlds.

THE MAGIC MIRROR

To deflect spells and for a general scrying glass, a magic mirror can be made. To make a magic mirror you will need the following items: a glass clock face four to twelve inches in diameter, crushed amber, crushed quartz and charcoal, clear varnish, filings of aluminum, gold, silver, iron, copper, lead, and tin, and some methylated spirit and black paint. Clean the glass with the methylated spirit and spray the convex side of the mirror with black paint. When the paint is dry apply a coat of clear varnish then sprinkle on the metals while the varnish is still wet, also the crushed amber, crystal, and charcoal, apply varnish to seal it (convex side also).

To charge the mirror, the Priestess holds it aloft at the northern gateway, facing toward the coven. The coven direct energy into the mirror while the Priestess makes the charge to the mirror:

May only good and pure intentions
Go forth into this mirror,
May it remove all evil from this place
And protect us from all harm.
In the name of the God and Goddess — So mote it be!

CHAPTER THREE

CASTING THE CIRCLE

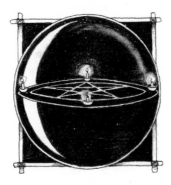

Wiccans believe that all things are cyclic and that all that dies is reborn. This is an ancient Shamanic belief that arises from watching the stars move in the heavens and the shoots spring from the cold earth. Wiccans do not fear death because they understand that in the cycle of life, it is necessary for the old to wither and die so that new growth can appear. Death is not an end but a transformation that leads to renewal.

The Wiccan circle also represents the womb of the mother and the protection it gives to the unborn child. The Wiccan circle, like the great neolithic stone circles, offers the protection of the womb of the Earth Mother to those within it. Thus the Wiccan circle may more appropriately be seen as a magical sphere, with one hemisphere rising up to the heavens, and the other buried beneath the earth.

The Wiccan circle is a mental and magical barrier that is erected to keep out unwanted influences and unwelcome spirits. In the Key of Solomon (from which Wicca borrows heavily) the formation of this magical circle is called the Conjuration, and the person who creates this magical barrier is called the Conjurer. In Wicca, these terms are also used, but the conjuration of the magic circle is called the Casting, and the person who casts it is called the Caster - casting meaning to throw up or out. A Wiccan circle can be cast by anyone, but the Priestess usually does it. This is because it requires a sustained mental effort to erect and maintain the invisible barrier. When a Wiccan circle is cast to protect those inside it from harm, the Priestess imagines herself to be surrounded by an invisible orb of blue light, half above and half beneath the ground.

In Wicca, a circle is also cast when it is necessary to draw power into the circle for a specific ritual. In this case, the circle is perceived as a cone of blue light, which is called the Cone of Power. This cone also contains the power that is raised within it until it is time for it to be released. The base of the cone is at floor level, but the apex of the cone is in the heavens. Power is raised within the cone through the spiral dance; this draws the power down into the cone in a spiral motion. The energy is then released straight upwards in a shaft of light.

Each cardinal point of the circle is marked with an elemental candle that corresponds to the colour of the quarter. Having the candles match their quarters allows the novice to know in which direction they are facing. It also helps to develop a familiarity with the elements; this is of great importance. Regardless of whether or not a circle has been marked out upon the floor, the elemental markers (watchtowers) are always erected. The traditional Wiccan circle is not usually marked out on the floor, it is purely mental and any friendly spirit is welcome to enter.

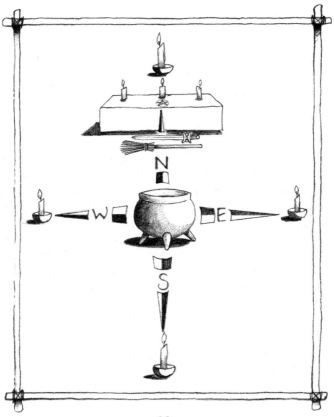

PREPARATION OF THE CIRCLE

In Wicca, there is a code of practice that must be adhered to:

1. All the ritual equipment and the place of worship must be cleaned thoroughly beforehand. Do not use poisons on eating utensils.

2. All participants must be bathed and wearing clean robes, except when skyclad (naked).

3. No shoes are to be worn in the place of worship. Socks are only worn for medical reasons.

4. Only menstruating women are allowed to wear underwear in the circle.

5. The red wine is sacred. No red wine is to be drunk before the ceremony of the cakes and wine. A little of the wine is always to be left in the chalice as an offering to the God and Goddess.

6. A twenty-four hour fast is to be observed before celebrating any of the Sabbats.

7. No watches are to be worn within the circle. Personal jewellery that is to be charged is allowed within the circle.

SAFE WORKING WITHIN THE CIRCLE

In order to work safely in the circle, the following procedures must be observed; failure to do so will result in a forfeit - if not an accident.

1. Robes of any colour can be worn in the circle, but robes that are loose or ill fitting can easily trip up the wearer or catch fire.

2. The temple or the area selected for the rite must be secured before the rite. Ensure that all doors are locked, and all lights, fires, and telephones are off, and that the house is empty. Once the circle is cast, there should be no interruptions.

3. All ritual equipment that is needed must be within the circle before the rite begins. The circle, once cast, is not to be left for any reason whatsoever.

4. All candles and naked flames must be safeguarded.

5. Good manners at all times and a positive mental attitude that is correct to the ritual must be adopted. No ill feelings must be brought into the circle. Be confident; state intentions clearly. Open and close down properly, and begin with "Let the ceremony begin."

6. The floor of the working area must be kept clear. Discarded clothing must be kept away from the area.

7. All callers and distractions during the ritual must be ignored unless it is of the utmost urgency. If the circle is to be broken, then it must be done in the correct manner.

8. When holding an outdoor ritual, select a location where you cannot be seen.

THE ARRANGEMENT OF THE ALTAR

The altar (see ritual equipment) is placed in the North or the Northeast of the room. For the full moon ritual, the table is to be covered with a black altar cloth that represents the night sky. On top of the altar, in the middle and to the rear, should be placed a silver or white candle. The colours silver and white represent the full Moon and they are burned during lunar rituals. The colours yellow and gold represent the Sun and they are burned during solar rituals. The brass pentacle (brass symbolizes the joining of male and female in the alloying of iron and copper) is placed in the centre of the altar and in front of the central candle. The salt for the blessing of the water is placed in a small triangle in the centre of the pentacle.

The scourge and the wand are laid to the left of the pentacle. To the right of the pentacle are laid the two daggers (the black handled athame and the white handled utility or purist knife - see ritual equipment.)

To the left of the central white or silver candle is placed a green candle (also in a candleholder). Green is a feminine colour associated with the planet Venus and therefore used to indicate the Goddess. This candle when lit represents the presence of the Goddess. To the right of the central candle is placed a red candle. Red is a masculine colour and when lit, it represents the presence of the Horned God.

A bowl containing some sand and a charcoal disk for the burning of loose incense must then be placed on the right-hand side of the altar, (eastern side) in front of the red candle. A bowl containing clean water must then be placed on the left side of the altar, (western side) in front of the green candle. A vase containing fresh flowers (flowers represent life) is to be placed on the altar in a vacant spot. You will also need a brass cup, a bell, tapers, matches, and any other items that might be crucial for the ritual.

On the floor in front of the altar should be placed large items such as the 'Sword of Power' and the Besom. Any bottles of wine and platters for cakes must be placed there also.

In the four directions of the compass are to be placed four squat candles that each sit in a bowl - having squat candles reduces the possibility of the candles being knocked over, and the dishes prevent the wax from dripping on the floor. Each of the candles is to be a different colour; these are elemental candles and are required for the watchtowers (see also candles).

At the eastern watchtower place a pale yellow candle to represent the element of air. At the southern watchtower place a red candle - red is the colour associated with masculinity and fire. At the western watchtower place a sea green or deep blue candle - aquamarine is the colour associated with water. At the northern portal place a brown or green candle to represent the element of earth.

Once all the precautions against interruptions have been taken, the watchtowers put in their places and the altar set-up; the casting of the circle may begin.

CASTING THE WICCAN CIRCLE

The circle is cast at all ceremonies regardless of the time of the month or year. The members of the coven assemble in the appointed place for the ritual and sit in a circle - male next to female, as is the ancient custom. They sit cross-legged or in the Egyptian scribe posture (sitting on the calves with the hands on the thighs, the back straight and the head slightly bowed) and wait quietly.

To begin the rite, the Priest lights the central candle and kneels before the altar (facing north). Placing his hands upon the altar, he mentally contacts the Gods (the altar is the focus point through which the God and Goddess are contacted). The Priest then lights the four elemental candles also with the taper, in a clockwise direction travelling with the sun, and returns to the altar. The Priest then lights the left and right altar candles, and addresses the coven

.

In the beginning there was the one light, the divine spark.
And from that one came the three,
So mote it be!

Note:
Walking clockwise, called deosil, in the same direction as the sun travels, is believed to aid the return of the sun. Walking anticlockwise, known as widdershins, travelling in the same direction as the stars, is believed to bring darkness and death.

The Priest then lights the incense and calls upon the Priestess who is waiting to enter the circle (if the circle is held outdoors, she waits outside the circle, if the circle is held indoors, she waits outside the room). The coven remain seated throughout:

All is in readiness, my Lady.
All that remains is for you to enter,
And to call upon the God and Goddess
To make this ground sacred with their presence.

Upon his call, the Priestess enters the room and the Priest retires to sit in his appointed place in the circle (in the East). The Priestess goes to the altar and contacts the Gods in the same manner as the Priest. After a short pause, she stands and takes up her athame to begin the consecration of the elements.

THE CONSECRATION OF THE ELEMENTS

The Priestess makes the banishing pentagram of water (see the pentagrams given in the illustrations) over the water and exorcises all impurities from within it:

I charge thee, O creature of the water,
That thou shall cast out all impurities
In the most holy and potent names of Cernunnos* and Aradia.

* Cernunnos is a word of Roman-British origin. The name Cernunnos is possibly a Romanisation of the name Herne, which is one of the earliest names by which the Horned (pronounced Horn-ed) God is known. The name is pronounced Ker-nunno, Ker-nunna, or Kar-ninna. The White Goddess is called Aradia and she is the daughter of the Goddess of the Moon (Diana). The Italian Witches of Tuscany say that she taught them the secrets of witchcraft. Some covens call them 'The

Lord and the Lady', which was their title in ancient Babylon. (Bel and Belit), and this title is perhaps the best way of describing them. The titles matter little; it is the mental image that accompanies the name that does matter.

Having spoken the charge, the Priestess then places the point of her athame into the salt and blesses it with the words:

Blessed be, O creature of earth,
I do consecrate thee and bless thee,
For thou art most pure.
In the most holy and potent names of Cernunnos and Aradia.

The Priestess then pours the salt into the water and, making a pentagram over it with her hand, she blesses the water:

O creature of water,
I do consecrate thee and bless thee,
For thou art most pure.
In the most holy and potent names of Cernunnos and Aradia.

The Priestess takes up her athame and goes to the centre of the circle where she stands to face north. The Priestess, holding her athame in both hands above her head, begins the circle conjuration.

The Priestess slowly lowers her athame until it points to the North. She focuses her gaze upon the point of her athame and imagines a blue light issuing from her blade. The Priestess then rotates clockwise drawing the imaginary blue protective line around the coven. While the Priestess casts the circle, she invokes the protection of the circle:

I conjure thee, O circle,
That thou shalt be a meeting place of love and joy and truth,
A shield against all wickedness and evil,
A boundary between the world of men
And the realm of the mighty ones,
A rampart and protection that shall contain and preserve
The power that we shall raise within thee.
Therefore I do bless thee and consecrate thee
In the most holy and potent names of Cernunnos and Aradia.

After the circle conjuration, the Priestess lowers her athame towards the floor - this is done to draw the protective barrier down to the floor. She then returns to the altar and lays down her athame. Taking up the blessed water the Priestess raises it to the North - in a salute to the

Gods, and begins to consecrate the circle with the holy water. She walks slowly around the circle in the direction of the sun (deosil) while sprinkling the holy water around the circle's edge (the water is sprinkled with the fingers of earth and water - the index finger and second fingers). Each time the Priestess approaches a member of the coven, she anoints them with the consecrated water.

> This procedure varies from coven to coven, sometimes she anoints them upon the forehead, sometimes she anoints them in the shape of an upright pentagram, forehead, left knee, right breast, left breast, right knee then forehead.

Once the circle has been purified with water, the Priestess returns to the altar and holding up the water, she proclaims to the Gods:

I declare this temple purified by earth and water.

The Priestess then takes up the incense and raises it in salute to the Gods beyond the northern gateway:

**I offer this incense as a sweet smelling offering
To the nostrils of the Gods,
May it please them!**

The Priestess inhales the incense and begins to cense the circle. Moving with slow sensual movements the Priestess spirals the incense upward. At each watchtower the Priestess pauses to raise the incense (as she does with all the other consecration items) in salute to the spirits of the quarter. Each time a member of the coven is approached, they look up and form the cup of acceptance with their hands. They then inhale the incense smoke as the Priestess passes - also to obtain inner purity. Once around the circle, the Priestess returns to the altar and proclaims that the circle has been purified:

I declare this temple purified by air!

The Priestess then raises the central candle (on the Estbats, the central candle is white or silver and on the Sabbats, the candle is gold or yellow) to the northern gateway. The Priestess then travels deosil once more around the circle; she pauses to raise the candle in silent salute to each watchtower as she passes. As the Priestess passes, the members of the coven raise their palms upwards, and lift their faces towards the light - in adoration of the light. Having completed this final journey, the Priestess returns once more to the altar and proclaims aloud:

I declare this temple purified by fire!

(A good way to remember the correct order of the consecration of the circle is to remember the lines of the witch's rune: "Earth and water, air and fire - work ye unto my desire!")

The Priestess puts down the central candle and takes up her athame; this time she erects the watchtowers to protect the circle. Beginning with the eastern watchtower, and moving slowly in a clockwise direction, the Priestess invokes each of the watchtowers in turn, calling upon the elemental spirits to guard her circle. At each watchtower she invokes the elements while drawing the invoking pentagram of the watchtower with her athame (see illustrations below).

At the eastern watchtower, the invoking pentagram of air is drawn with the athame and the following invocation is spoken:

**Ye Lords and Guardians of the
Watchtower of the east,
I do summon, stir, and call ye up, to
Witness here our rite,
In the most holy and potent names
of Cernunnos and Aradia!**

AIR

FIRE

At the southern watchtower the invoking pentagram of fire is drawn with the athame and the following invocation is given:

**Ye Lords and Guardians of the
Watchtower of the south!
I do summon, stir, and call ye up,
To witness here our rite,
In the most holy and potent names
of Cernunnos and Aradia!**

When using a pentagram to invoke, start from the point marked "I" and continue in the direction of the arrow. To banish, begin at point "B" and move in the opposite direction, as marked.

At the western watchtower, the invoking pentagram of water is drawn with the athame and the following invocation given:

> **Ye Lords and Guardians of the**
> **Watchtower of the west!**
> **I do summon, stir, and call ye up,**
> **To witness here our rite.**
> **In the most holy and potent names**
> **of Cernunnos and Aradia!**

EARTH

At the northern watchtower the invoking pentagram of earth is drawn with the athame and the following invocation spoken:

> **Ye Lords and Guardians of the**
> **Watchtower of the north,**
> **I do summon, stir, and call ye up,**
> **To witness here our rite.**
> **Makest thou a gateway**
> **Wherein only the Horned God**
> **And most gracious Goddess may enter.**
> **In the most holy and potent names of**
> **Cernunnos and Aradia!**

The Priestess returns to the altar and lays down her athame, she then addresses the coven:

> **In the name of the God and Goddess,**
> **I now declare this circle open!**
> **May we remain safe between the worlds**
> **Until the spell be broken.**
> **Let the ceremony begin!**

The Priestess then calls to the coven:

> **O Come, ye of the joyous craft,**
> **And join me in the sacred dance!**

RAISING POWER IN THE WHEEL DANCE

The circle having been cast, the coven must now raise the power for the magical working. In Wicca there are eight ways of raising power (see the eightfold way). In the normal full moon circle working, (Estbat) most covens use the wheel dance. To enact the wheel dance, the members of the coven join hands in the centre of the circle and dance clockwise. Slowly, with ever-increasing speed, the wheel begins to rotate. As the coven dance faster and faster, they chant the witch's rune:

THE WITCH'S RUNE

Darksome night and shining moon.
East then south then west then north,
Hearken to the witches' rune,
Here we come to call ye forth!
Earth and water, air and fire,
Wand, and pentacle, and sword,
Work ye unto my desire.
Hearken ye unto my word!
Cords and censer scourge and knife,
Powers of the witch's blade,
Awaken all ye unto life.
Come ye as the charm is made!

Queen of heaven, queen of hell,
Horned hunter of the night,
Lend your power unto my spell.
And work my will by magic rite.
By all the power of land and sea
By all the light of moon and sun
As I do will so mote it be.
Chant the spell and be it done!

(At this point in the ritual, some covens opt to chant in rhyme the intention of the rite instead of the chorus.)

Chorus.   Eco, Eco, Azarak, Eco, Eco, Zomelak,
                   Eco, Eco, Ka-nina, Eco, Eco, Aradia.

(The chorus is always repeated three times)

The chant and the dance increase in vigour until the wheel is spinning. When the Priest and Priestess decide that enough power has been raised, the Priestess will call "Down!" At this call, the coven immediately stop the dance and drop to the floor. After a short break for the coven to recuperate, the ceremony of the cakes and wine is enacted.

THE CEREMONY OF THE CAKES AND WINE

This rite is enacted to give honour to the dying God of vegetation who sacrifices himself for humanity every year, and to give thanks to the God and Goddess for their good favour. The ceremony of the cakes was enacted at the end of the harvesting of the crops and the ceremony of the wine was performed at the end of the grape harvesting. At the end of the harvest season, an image of the God of vegetation is made from bread (John Barleycorn) and baked in an oven. The bread in the shape of the God is then shared out among the people so they can partake of his divinity.

To begin the ceremony of the cakes and wine, the Priest and Priestess approach the altar. The Priest takes up the red wine and the Priestess kneels before the Priest with the chalice. The Priestess then raises the chalice (which is the symbol of the Goddess) up to the Priest. The Priest fills her chalice with red wine. The Priestess hands the cup to the Priest and he kneels down beside the Priestess. The Priestess then stands and taking up her athame in both hands she raises it above the chalice (point downward). The Priest holds the wine up to the Priestess. The Priestess, still holding her athame aloft, begins the invocation and plunges her athame into the cup. The Priestess makes the charge:

I call upon the God and Goddess to witness here our rite,
And to lift the veil between us.
As the cup is to the female, so the athame is to the male,
And may their conjunction bring great blessedness for us all.

The uniting of the athame with the chalice (lance and grail) represents the conjoining of the God with the Goddess. Wiccans that truly understand the nature of this rite will know that the phallic wand is the symbol of the Horned God not the athame. Therefore, the wand should technically be used with the chalice and not the athame - the use of the athame instead of the wand, was possibly conceived to avoid offending onlookers or to veil the nature of the rite. For those that feel that gender roles in Wicca need rebalancing, this ritual may be performed with the Priestess kneeling with the chalice while the Priest wields the athame.

After the invocation, the athame is laid down upon the altar. The Priest then rises and the Priestess drinks from the cup first. The Priestess then offers the cup to the Priest and he accepts the cup with a kiss and the password:

From me to thee, blessed be!

The Priest returns the blessing: **Blessed be!**

(In the craft of Wicca, all things are passed in this manner.)

After the Priest has drunk from the cup, he then hands the wine to the nearest maiden of the coven - also with a kiss and a blessing. The wine is then passed around the circle and each person drinks from the cup. The wine is not to be placed upon the floor, and no person is to consume more than his or her fair share under penalty of forfeit. If the Priest and the Priestess consider that someone is taking too long, they will start counting downwards. At the end of the countdown from 10 if the cup has not been passed on, a penalty is awarded and a forfeit made. At the end of the rite, there must always be a little wine left in the cup as a libation to the God and Goddess.

THE BLESSING OF THE FOOD

After the ceremony of the wine, the blessing of the cakes is performed. The Priest holds the offering aloft, while he kneels before the Priestess. The Priestess takes up her athame from the altar and also raises it aloft, (it was always the Priestess who took the life of the Green King) the Priestess then gives thanks to the God and Goddess:

Great God and Goddess,
We thank thee for thy blessing most bountiful,
Without which we would not be.
Blessed be!

Personally, I find the following variation by Doreen Valiente more sincere and to the point.

I call upon the God and Goddess to witness our sacrifice,
With pleasure and understanding,
And to know that we do this in memory of those
Who gave their lives willingly so that others would live on;
And in the partaking of this bread and wine,
We too shall become one with the land.

The Priestess pierces the cake with her athame and cuts it; she then withdraws her athame, and lays it down upon the altar. The Priestess then gives a portion of the cake to the Priest with a kiss and a blessing:

From me to thee, blessed be!

The Priest in return, breaks off some of the cake and hands it to the Priestess - also with a kiss and the blessing. The members of the coven then each partake of the food and drink while passing it clockwise around the circle also with a kiss and a blessing. A little of the wine and food must always be left over for the libation at the end of the circle. After the coven has partaken of the food, the Priestess then asks the coven:

Is there any work to be done?

If the answer is yes, any magical work that is fitting for the time of the month is then done; there is no magical work done on the Sabbats, which are purely celebrations and an enactment of the nature myths.

THE CLOSING OF THE CIRCLE

At the end of the ritual, the Priest and Priestess go to the altar and take up their athames. They then go to each of the watchtowers in turn and draw the banishing pentagram for each watchtower while they dismiss the guardians of the circle. The coven stands behind them while they do this.

At the east they call:

**Ye Lords and guardians of the watchtower of the east
I do thank thee for attending this our rite,
And ere' ye depart to your lovely and airy realm
I do bid ye - hail and farewell!**

At the south they call:

**Ye Lords and guardians of the watchtower of the south
I do thank thee for attending this our rite,
And ere' ye depart to your lovely and fiery realm.
I do bid ye - hail and farewell!**

At the west the farewell is given:

> **Ye Lords and guardians of the watchtower west**
> **I do thank thee for attending this our rite,**
> **And ere' ye depart to your lovely and watery realm.**
> **I do bid ye - hail and farewell!**

At the north, the farewell is given:

> **Ye Lords and guardians of the watchtower of the North**
> **I do thank thee for attending this our rite,**
> **And ere' ye depart to your lovely and earthly realm.**
> **I do bid ye - hail and farewell!**

As the charge is given, the coven echo:

> **Hail and farewell!**

The Priestess must then go to the circle's rim and cut the invisible cord with her athame, while the Priest puts out the elemental candles. The Priestess leaves the Priest to extinguish the red and green altar candles leaving only the central candle burning. After a short silence the Priest extinguishes the central candle with the words:

> **In the beginning there was the one light,**
> **And from that one light came the three.**
> **And from the three came the one,**
> **Thus and evermore shall it be!**

The Priest then faces the coven:

> **The rite has ended - I declare this circle closed!**

LEAVING THE CIRCLE

Once the circle has been cast, it should never be left until it has been dissolved. To suddenly leave the circle (this is called breaking the circle) could result in great mental and physical harm to the group involved in the working. If a circle must be broken, then there are ways of mentally enforcing the barrier. There are occasions when it becomes necessary to leave the circle; this can be accomplished in several ways. One way of leaving the circle is to place the besom across the edge of the circle and jump over it. Another way is to cut an imaginary opening in the barrier with the athame. The person who wishes to leave must open the veil as he would open curtains.

Once the hole has been opened, it can then be stepped through. Once through, the hole must be closed by drawing the two edges of the invisible cut together. To re-enter the circle, the procedure is the same. Some covens position two markers at the northern gateway; to rend the veil, they place the besom across the gateway. Once the besom has been removed, the line is redrawn with the athame. Those groups that mark their boundary with salt redraw the line.

THE LIBATION

After the circle has been closed, the libation to the Gods is to be performed. For the libation, a little of the wine and bread are to be returned to the ground as an offering to the God and Goddess. In times of old, however, the libation was offered to the Gods before the people partook of their share:

> **Great God and Goddess, we do give thanks to thee,**
> **For thine offering most bounteous.**
> **For without which we would not be. Blessed be!**

The food and drink are then to be taken outside and returned to the ground. All are to bow before departing.

CASTING THE OUTDOOR CIRCLE.

Sometimes, if a suitable place can be found, it is possible to hold the full moon rituals and Sabbats outdoors. Unfortunately in modern times, privacy is hard to find - as are like-minded people who will let witches conduct their ceremonies on their land. If a suitable place can be found, possibly a stone circle, a sheltered grove or just a dry, flat, sheltered and secluded spot, the following items will be required to help in the construction of the circle: Two pointed daggers, a nine-foot length of string, a packet of matches, some firelighters, some lighter fuel, a bundle of kindling, four barbecue torches for the elemental markers, and two torches for the gateway markers (if you are using them).

To mark out the circle, the Priest must plunge the first dagger point into the ground in the centre of the appointed place. The nine-foot string is then tied to the handles of both daggers. The perimeter of the circle is then marked out in a clockwise direction (while travelling with the sun) with the tip of the second dagger. A four-foot gap is to be left in the North as a gateway and marked with the torches (while the circle is marked out, the coven is to wait patiently to the Northeast - outside the circle).

The Magical Needs fire must then be built in the centre of the circle using the firewood. The fire is lit to impart warmth and light to the circle. Upon the eve of the Sabbats, a Belfire is lit. The majority of covens do not have access to land for outdoor ceremonies, so they build a small fire in the cauldron, but for most of the indoor rites, they use candles to replace the ancient Belfires and temple braziers.

Once the fire has been lit, the torches that are to be used as watchtowers are planted at each of the points of the four winds (east, south, west, north). This done, the coven enters the circle carrying all the equipment needed for the rite, and awaits the arrival of the Priestess. The Priest then calls upon the Priestess to enter the circle as is done in the normal circle working. Once the Priestess has entered the circle, the Priest closes the gateway of the circle with one of the daggers (the athame is never used for this purpose). The Priestess then declares to the coven:

The circle is closed behind me,
May we remain safe between the worlds
Until the spell be broken.
In the name of the God and Goddess,
I now declare this circle open.

The Priest takes his appointed position in the East and the circle is then cast (and eventually closed) in the prescribed manner. The Priest ends the rite with:

The rite has ended!
I now declare this circle closed!

INTRODUCTION TO THE CIRCLE

It is the practice to welcome newcomers into the circle - don't confuse this with the first degree initiation. The newcomers wait outside the room while the circle is cast. A gateway is then made in the circle so that each newcomer in turn can be led blindfold into the room. This practice stems from the days when the newcomer was not to know the location of the meeting place, or the identity of those who were there. Each newcomer is then pushed from behind towards the circle where the Priest or Priestess greets him or her. The Priestess greets all new male guests and the Priest greets all new female guests - in the craft of Wicca everything is done male to female and female to male. At the circle's rim the Priest or Priestess asks the newcomer:

Who hast brought thee to the sacred circle?

The newcomer replies:

I do not know, I did not see them!

The Priest or Priestess then whispers to them:

I give thee two passwords - in perfect love and perfect trust!

The Priest or Priestess then grasps the newcomer by the shoulders
and says:

I give thee a third!

The newcomer to the circle is then kissed upon the lips. The
newcomer is then spun into the circle with a clockwise motion
imitating the passage of the sun. The Priest or Priestess then says
unto them:

In this way we are brought into the circle!

The newcomer may then work with the coven as a guest for three
months.

CHAPTER FOUR

THE RITES OF WICCA

THE RITE OF CONSECRATION

A ll magical and ritual items must be cleansed, purified and charged before they are used. This consecration should, if possible, be performed by someone of the opposite sex to the owner. After the item has been duly consecrated and charged, it is then given back to the rightful owner in the prescribed manner.

Note:
Where possible, men and women work together as pairs. This brings the group closer together and increases harmony. It eradicates any sexual discrimination that might arise, and because of the chemistry that exists between a man and a woman, the power that they raise is greater than that of a single person, or a group of one sex. Through the unification of polar opposites, a balance can be achieved.

The item is first cleansed through the elements of earth and water (this is done to remove any impurities). This can be achieved by sprinkling the item three times with consecrated water (three is the number of the moon). The declaration of purity is then recited while the item is cleansed:

I purify thee through earth and water.

The next step is to purify the item through the element of air. The item is passed three times in a clockwise direction through the rising smoke of the incense burner, again with the declaration of purity:

I purify thee through air.

The item is then purified through the element of fire. To accomplish this, the object is spiralled clockwise three times through a candle flame with the declaration of purity:

I purify thee through fire.

The purification of the elements completed, the item is then blessed:

I do consecrate thee and bless thee,
For thou art most pure.
In the most holy and potent names of Cernunnos and Aradia!

The consecrated item is then placed upon the pentacle and an invoking pentagram is made over it with the athame. The athame is then pointed at the centre of the item which is charged with an imaginary blue light that issues from the tip of the athame. A charge is then made to invoke power into the item:

I do conjure thee, O (name of the item).
In the names of the God and Goddess,
That thou shalt receive the power
For the purpose for which thou shalt be used,
And for thy purpose, I will all my power into thee!

If another has consecrated the item, the consecrator and the owner turn to face one another. They stand knee to knee, lip to lip, breast to breast, and toe to toe. The item is then placed between their breasts and they embrace tightly. The consecrator tells the recipient of the item:

Be ready to catch the consecrated item when we part!

The owner must then catch the item as they part. If the item falls to the floor, the entire consecration ritual will have to be re-enacted. This practice cannot be used with large objects. The item may then be left upon an item that has already been charged to receive a further charge.

CONSECRATING IMAGES

In the craft of Wicca a magical image is regarded as nothing less than a real person, and anything that is done to the image will also result in the same thing happening to the person whom the image represents. An image or likeness (as it is also called) can be constructed from clay, wax, cloth, metal, wood, bread, or any other suitable substance that is nearby - in Wicca most magical images are made from wax. Any personal items belonging to the person whom the image is to represent may be incorporated into the image when it is constructed - to help create a psychic link between the recipient of the spell and the caster. These items can be worked into pliable substances or hidden in secret compartments in solid images. Any item of clothing, hair, nail parings, shoes or jewellery can be used and hidden in an image (the ancient witches also used garments belonging to their patient or victim and depending upon the purpose of the rite, they burnt them, rent them, or trampled them underfoot). Regardless of what substance is used for the construction of an image, (these are also called poppets, likenesses, dolls, fith-faths and effigies) for that image to gain life, it must first receive life.

Once the image is a reasonable likeness to the person it is to represent, it must then be attached to your waist using a red thread as an umbilical cord. The umbilical cord is then cut at the moment of its birth and life must then be breathed into the image with a straw. Blow three times and make the following charge:

As life was breathed into us,
So shall life be breathed into you — So mote it be!

The breast of the image is touched with the tip of the athame and the image is to be imagined warm and alive. The image is then given a name and introduced to the watchtowers first, then to the God and Goddess. At each watchtower the name of the image is declared with the following charge for recognition.

At the eastern watchtower say:

Ye Lords and guardians of the watchtowers of the east
Recognize this image as a likeness of _____ (name).

At the southern watchtower say:

Ye Lords and guardians of the watchtowers of the south
Recognize this image as a likeness of _____ (name).

At the western watchtower say:

Ye Lords and guardians of the watchtowers of the west
Recognize this image as a likeness of _____ (name).

At the northern watchtower say:

Ye Lords and guardians of the watchtowers of the north
Recognize this image as a likeness of _____ (name).

At the altar say:

Great God and Goddess, recognize ye,
This image as a likeness of _____ (name)

The image is then considered to be alive and any magical work may then be performed upon it. After an image is finished with, it must be released. This process is almost the same as the rite of consecration. To dissolve an image, the image is again shown to the watchtowers and then to the God and Goddess. This time a declaration of dissolution is made:

Ye Lords and guardians of the watchtowers
Of the east / south / west / north,
Recognize this image as no longer a likeness of ____ (name).

The light within the breast of the image is then imagined to fade away leaving the image cold and lifeless. The image can then be dismantled in the same way it was made without anything unpleasant happening to the person whom the image once represented. If it is a wax image, it must be gently melted through heat. A clay image must be dissolved in water, never broken up.

CANDLE MAGIC

In Wicca, candles are used for casting spells. In candle-magic, the size of the candle is unimportant, so is the period of time that a candle burns for. However, the colours are important and each colour has a link with a certain type of energy. Therefore, any candle that is to be burned must be of the correct colour for the purpose of the rite.

SETTING UP THE ALTAR

To cast a candle spell, the altar must have a solitary candle of the correct planetary colour upon it. This candle is the focus point of the ritual. If at all possible, the colour of the candle, the altar cloth and any robes worn should match. Any incense that is to be burned must consist of the correct planetary ingredients. The ritual must also be performed upon the correct date and time given for the planet.

BLACK CANDLES.

The colour black represents darkness and the planet Saturn. Black candles are generally burned to cast spells of malice, restriction and death, but black candles can also be burned to acquire knowledge and to obtain safe passage while travelling in the spirit realms.

RED CANDLES

Red candles represent the God of Fire, the planet Mars, desire, the masculine, and the element of fire. Red candles are burned to cause strife, invoke the God of War, draw courage, obtain objects of desire, and summon fire elementals - the salamanders.

GREEN CANDLES

Green candles represent the Goddess, the planet Venus, and the feminine. They are burned to obtain love, bring compassion, and ease heartache.

BLUE CANDLES

Blue candles represent the planet Jupiter, the healing powers and the fairy-folk. Blue candles are burned for spells of healing, obtaining greatness and invoking the fairy folk.

WHITE AND SILVER CANDLES

White candles represent purity, the moon, magic, and the power of light. White candles are burned for spells of protection and in matters of divination.

GOLD AND YELLOW CANDLES

Gold and old yellow candles represent the warmth of the sun; they are burned for spells to obtain wealth, health and harmony.

SEA GREEN CANDLES

Sea green and turquoise candles represent the elemental of water and rejuvenation. These candles are burned to attract the powers of Neptune and the water sprites - the mermaids.

PALE YELLOW, RAINBOW, & TWO-TONE CANDLES

Pale yellow, rainbow and two-tone (black and white) candles represent the planet Mercury and the elemental of air and they are burned to attract the powers of Mercury and the sylphs (fairies).

BROWN AND DARK GREEN CANDLES

Brown and dark green candles represent the elemental of earth, and they are burned to attract the gnomes who can reveal the whereabouts of buried treasure.

THE CANDLE SPELL

To cast a candle spell, you must first choose a candle of the correct colour. Carve into the candle the wish that you would like to come true. The wish must be written from the top downwards, spiralling around the candle clockwise to the bottom. While this is done, the following spell should be spoken:

> **Upon this candle I shall write,**
> **What I require of you tonight.**
> **Gracious Goddess of the moon,**
> **I pray that you will grant it soon.**

The candle is to be anointed with accumulator oil (i.e., rectified amber or an essential oil that is compatible with the working), which will assist the candle to draw power to itself. The candle is then placed in a holder to ensure that it does not fall over while it is alight. The candle is then lit with the spell, and put somewhere safe to burn down (the entire candle must burn away for the spell to be passed regardless of its size). When the candle has died out, the wish is passed.

ELEMENTAL CANDLES

In Wicca, four candles (each a different colour) are placed on the inside of the circle's boundary at each of the watchtowers. These candles are called the elemental candles and when these candles are lit, they represent the presence of the elemental creatures that guard the circle. The elemental candles are put in place before the circle is cast and they are placed in the following order: Yellow in the East, Red in the South, Sea green in the West, and brown in the North.

THE ALTAR CANDLES

In Wicca there are three other candles that are used in circle working. These are placed upon the altar and they represent the presence of the God, the Goddess, and the Moon or the Sun. The central or middle candle represents the Sun during solar rituals and the Moon during lunar rituals. Regardless of the rite, the central candle is always higher than the other two candles.

CORD MAGIC

Cords or ropes have long been used as magical tools. The ancients believed that each person was allotted a length of rope at birth by the three fates. It was the belief that the tying of a knot in a length of rope (with an ill wish) could shorten or cause problems in a person's life. Wiccans also practice a modern form of these ancient knot-spells and they call it cord magic.

For the casting of knot spells, the circle is cast in the usual manner and cords are given to those who do not possess their own. The coven is seated male next to female, as is the custom when working in the circle. The pentacle is placed in the middle of the circle to mark the centre.

The person who sits in the South gives the other end of their cord to the person who is sitting opposite them. The person sitting in the North loops their cord around the other cord, and gives the other end to the person who is sitting opposite. This continues until each person holds the end of a cord. The cords must all join in the centre - this forms the hub of the wheel (in some covens the person who sits at a 90-degree angle is given the end of the cord and not the person opposite).

To begin the rite, the Priestess places her foot on the cords trapping them to the pentacle. The coven are then instructed that when her foot is lifted, they are to pull the cords taut, then while keeping the cords taut, they are to each tie eight knots in the cord. At the indication that the coven is ready, the Priestess calls: "Pull" and lifts her foot. As each knot is tied, the intention of the rite must be held firmly fixed in the mind of the coven. Those who are slacking may find themselves lightly scourged. The centre of the cords must remain over the pentacle while the following chant is recited. As each knot is tied the coven call:

> **Knot of one, spell begun.**
> **Knot of two, my wish come true.**
> **Knot of three, it shall be.**
> **Knot of four, 'tis strengthened more.**
> **Knot of five, spell may thrive.**
> **Knot of six, the spell I fix.**
> **Knot of seven, gates of heaven,**
> **Knot of eight, I seal thy fate.**

Once all the knots are tied, the Priestess places her foot back on the cords and 'earths' them to the pentacle. The cords are then collected up and put on the altar. The knots are not untied until the next full moon. Once untied, the cords are cleansed through the incense smoke and given back to their owners. The above ritual is typical of an Alexandrian coven ritual. Solitary witches can also cast knot spells by knotting their cord over the rising smoke from the incense burner.

COUNTERING A KNOT SPELL

A Priest or Priestess can counter another witch's knot spell by using cords that are already knotted. In this ritual, the knots are tied in the cord before the ritual begins. These knots represent the knots that the witch has already tied. To undo her spell, the cord is simply unknotted during the ritual. As the knots are untied, a counterspell is recited:

> **Knot of one, spell undone.**
> **Knot of two, spell undo.**
> **Knot of three, it shall not be.**
> **Knot of four, 'tis weakened more.**
> **Knot of five, spell won't thrive.**
> **Knot of six, spell unfix.**
> **Knot of seven, stars in heaven,**
> **Knot of eight, tis to your gate!**
> (Knot of eight sends the spell back)

THE RITE OF HEALING

Healing is always performed before the God and Goddess and takes place in both the physical world, and in the spiritual world - this includes all forms of healing. All methods of healing can be performed either upon the patient or upon an image of the patient. Before and after giving any healing treatment, the healer should wash his or her hands.

PSYCHIC HEALING

Psychic healing is sometimes called faith healing. Faith healing requires that the patient must believe in the healer. In this way the patients use their own latent energies to heal themselves. In psychic healing, the patient does not have to believe in the healer; the healing energy comes directly from the healer. Psychic healing is given to the patient by what is called the 'laying on of hands'. In this way, many illnesses can be treated.

The power to heal is deep within us all and must be called up. Many of us have this gift, some people are natural healers, others have to learn how to heal. Many healers are able to see the colour of the patient's aura along with the afflicted area of the body (the colour and depth of the aura changes over the afflicted area).

To draw out pain and sickness, a healer places their hands over the patient. A psychic healer usually draws out illness by mentally (not physically) pulling with their right hand. They are also capable of giving healing by 'pushing' with their left hand (this technique is reversible by pushing with the right hand and pulling with the left hand). Pain and sickness can be drawn out of the patient (most psychic healers experience pain in their arm when doing this) but the healer must take care not to absorb it and become ill themselves. To avoid absorbing anything that they have drawn out of the patient, they 'shake' off any illness with a flicking motion of the hand, as if they have something stuck to it.

The healer, having drawn out the pain, must then 'patch' in the damaged aura over the afflicted area using his or her own healthy aura. This is done by placing the hands over the weak section and projecting a healthy aura into it. This is to help prevent any other illness from entering the body. Dion Fortune in her book Psychic Self-Defence us informs us that weak spots in the aura are open gateways that can allow us to be psychically attacked.

In Wicca, if the patient who is to be given healing is not present, they can still be given healing through the use of a photograph or an image; this technique is called "absent healing".

ABSENT HEALING

To perform absent healing for all manner of illnesses, the following items are required:

> A healing wand
> A blue candle
> An image made from blue playdough
> or a photograph of the patient
> A bowl of water
> A rose or quartz crystal.

For the rite of absent healing the circle is cast in the usual manner. When the time for the healing work arrives, the image is to be brought to life in the traditional way (see the consecration of the image). The Priestess then goes to the altar and removes the rose quartz or crystal (if one has been used) from the water and raises the bowl of water in both hands. The Priest then takes up either his athame or the caduceus and invokes the healing powers of the God and Goddess into the water. The Priest calls aloud:

> **I do bless thee, O creature of water,**
> **And I do charge thee with the sacred powers of healing,**
> **In the most holy and potent names**
> **Of Cernunnos and Aradia!**

The Priestess then places the water in the centre of the circle and the Priest puts his athame down on the altar. The Priestess then takes up the image of the patient and brings it to the bowl of water. The image of the patient is then bathed with the ritually charged water. Each member of the coven in turn (beginning with the Priestess), bathes the image while a spell for healing is recited.

> I bathe thee O image of (name),
> In the cool waters of healing
> For the cleansing of thy soul,
> And as the water shall run away from thine image,
> So shall thy pain and affliction melt away from thee.
> Thy wounds shall be healed, and pain and misery,
> Headache and fever, sickness and disease
> Shall no longer haunt thee,
> Thou shalt once more be healthy and well!

As the water runs off the image, the affliction is to be visualised by the group melting away into the water. The image is then seen surrounded by a healthy clean blue aura. After the image has been given healing it is placed back on the altar. The image must then be kept safe until all the healing work is successful - healing is sometimes given more than once. Once the healing is completed, the image is dissolved.

TREATING CANCERS AND TUMORS

Many people turn to Wicca for help in the treatment of cancer, generally regarded as incurable by orthodox medicine. In the Craft of Wicca, cancer is curable, though not if it is karmic. I have seen it done. For this particular type of healing you will need all the items quoted in the list for normal healing, also a pair of tweezers, and some whole cloves (the image must be pierced with whole cloves and the quartz placed in the water before the rite begins).

The circle is cast and the image is to be brought to life in the traditional manner. The water is blessed and the water and the image are brought to the centre of the circle and the coven gather around. The clove buds represent the cancer or lump that afflicts the patient. During the rite, the members of the coven are to each remove one of the clove buds (with the tweezers) while imagining they are extracting the disease from the patient. The clove buds are then to be burned in the candle flame while the destruction of the affliction is visualised. The image of the patient is then to be bathed with the ritually charged water to heal them. As the image is bathed, the affliction is to be visualised as being washed away and the image should be seen as surrounded by a clean blue aura. As the Priestess bathes the image she recites the spell:

I bathe thee in the cool waters of healing
For the cleansing of thy soul,
And as the water shall run away from thine image
So shall it carry away thy pain and misery,
Thou shalt once more be healthy and well,
Free from affliction!

Healing crystals such as clear crystal 'points' are also used in Wicca for the purpose of healing. Crystals and gemstones were thought by the ancient Gnostics to possess healing properties. In crystal healing, the crystals or gemstones are stroked over, or placed upon, the afflicted part of the body to cure the ailment. Sometimes the water in which crystals and gemstones are steeped is drunk to provide a cure. The healing practices used with gemstones and crystals can also be applied in absent healing.

THE RITE OF KARMA

Internal disputes are settled by invoking the God of Karma. Once the circle has been cast, the accused is brought before the coven and given a fair trial. All that sit in judgment must swear upon the God and Goddess to be unbiased in their decisions and those that give evidence must swear to tell only the truth. For the rite of karma, the Sword of Power is required. The ritual must be performed during the full moon. The accused must be present or at least have someone to speak for them. The circle is cast in the usual manner, and the Priest begins the rite by raising up the sword of power. The Priest calls aloud:

Now begins the rite of karma!
Let only the truth be spoken, Let only the truth be heard!

The Priest then calls for the accuser:

Who among us has been wronged?

The accuser steps forward and speaks of the crime. The accused is then called forth:

(Name), Thou hast been accused of (crime).
Swear now upon thy oath as a witch
Before the God and Goddess
That thou shall speak only the truth.
For by the sword, shall ye be duly judged!

The accused then replies:

> I swear on my oath as a witch
> To tell only the truth, before the God and Goddess!

The accused tells their side of the story. The coven then decide upon the verdict and what action if any to take. The accused is then 'Judged by the Sword'. The Priest raises the sword and invokes the laws of Karma.

> The Three Fates we have known,
> The mother, maiden and crone,
> Urd, Verdandi, and Skuld they be!
> Come ye maids who much do know,
> Clotho, Lachis, Atropo,
> Three from the hall beneath the tree,
> One named WAS, and BEING next,
> The third is named - WHAT SHALL BE!
> As for the blessed, the path is laid,
> So must evil be repaid.
> To those wronged, thy blessings give,
> For by thy grace, we all do live.

The Priest is to then face the coven and speak the charge:

> We do find thee_____ guilty/
> Not guilty of the charges against thee!

The Priest then gives the charge:

> In times past, those found guilty of serious crimes
> Were banished from the community.
> The blessings of the God and Goddess were denied to them
> And none would give them food or shelter
> In these times we need not be so harsh
> But, as ye have sown, so shall ye reap
> Good fortune or ill, according to your merit
> For all will receive their just due on the wheel of karma!

At the end of the rite, the sword is sheathed and the circle is dissolved.

THE RITE OF HANDFASTING

Handfasting is the joining of man and woman in wedlock with the blessing of the God and Goddess. The rite of Handfasting can be performed on any of the great Sabbaths, except for Halloween, but it is usually performed at Midsummer or Beltane. Handfasting lasts for a trial period of a year and a day. After that, if they so wish it, the couple can be handfasted for life.

For the ceremony, the bride is to wear a white dress with a veil. The bride's dress is to be fastened at the left breast with a blue brooch so that when the brooch is removed, the left breast is bared. The bride also wears a garter with her athame in it.

Something old, something new, something borrowed and something blue is still the custom here. The bridegroom is to wear a leather belt, leather gloves, a dark robe, a white scarf, a dagger, and carry a sword. The bride and groom are to spend the twenty-four hours prior to the ritual apart in the company of members of the same sex. The men, in times past, would have gone on a last hunt - the stag night.

It is the custom even in pagan weddings that the couple should not see each another before the wedding as it is thought unlucky. In the morning, the maids are to gather flowers for the bride, the altar and the reception room. The groom is to buy the food. The best man is to ensure that the banquet is in readiness and the flowers are in the cauldron and on the marital bed.

THE CEREMONY

The circle is to be cast in the prescribed manner with the bride and groom absent from the room. The Priest and the Priestess are to face the coven and proclaim the intention of the rite:

Maidens of the Goddess and merry men of the forest,
Open the circle for the two who come, who would be one.

The coven is to part to make way for the bride and groom to enter. The groom enters first while music is played. The men must bow to the bride, and the maidens must bow to the groom. The coven is to close behind them and the Priestess is to invoke the Goddess:

There is magic to be done here, magic of love.
This place is calling thee O Goddess.
Come to us from thy realm of beauty to this thy holy circle,
A place of thine, no less pleasing.
Hear then, O gracious Lady, and bring thy lovely person
To bless the two who have come here.

The Priest then invokes the God:

There is magic to be done here, magic of love,
This place is calling thee, O Horned One.
Come to us from your wild land of sunshine and forest,
To this holy gathering in a place of thine own, no less wild.
Hear then, O bringer of great cheer,
Draw thy rough magic
And bless the two who have come here.

The Priestess then anoints the bride:

Thou art consecrated before the Goddess.

The Priest then anoints the groom:

Thou art consecrated before the God.

The Priest and Priestess then address the couple:

Kneel and receive thy charge.

The Priestess then holds the cup above the bride and charges her:

Thou shalt be the star that rises from the sea,
Thou shalt bring to man the dreams of his destiny,
Thou shalt bring the tides that flow to the soul of man.
The secrets of the moon belong to thee,
As ye the Goddess can see in me.

The Priest then raises his wand above the groom with the charge:

In thee may the Horned God return to play,
The shepherd of wild things along the way.
Forgotten are the ways of sleep and night,
Lead thy flock into the light.
Open the door to dreams,
Whereby all men come unto thee,
Herder of wild things one with him be.

The Priestess is then to ask them both to rise and say unto them:

It has been said that you do both wish Handfasting
Before the God and Goddess, is this so?

The couple says:

Aye

The Priestess then draws her athame and places the point into the two rings that lie on the altar. (One on top of the other) The Priest then addresses the groom:

If thou dost truly desire to marry this woman,
Surrender to her thy weapon,
So it may be used in her service.

The groom removes his sword and kneels offering the bride his sword:

Gracious and lovely one, accept all that I have,
The farthest at thy service!

The bride takes the sword and hands it to the Priestess who gives it to a maiden. The Priestess then addresses the bride:

If thou dost truly wish to marry this man,
Then give to him thy blue jewel, for his possession alone.

The bride curtseys and indicates her brooch to the groom:

Thou who art handsome and strong,
Accept my jewel, my treasure, for it is all I own.

The groom is to remove her brooch revealing her left breast and hand it to the Priest. The bride then rises from her curtsey and the Priest gives the groom her brooch.

The rings are given to the couple and they are to place the rings on each other's fingers. The couple then join hands and the Priest ties their hands together with a cord announcing:

Thy hands are fastened, now thou art one.

The couple kiss and the Priest addresses the coven:

Goddess maidens, and merry men,
Break the circle, that the groom
May take the bride to the wedding chamber.

The circle parts allowing the groom to carry the bride across the threshold. Merriment follows, and after a time, the circle is dissolved. Three hours later, the coven calls upon the couple to attend the feast. The groom makes a speech, which is followed by the feast. The cauldron is filled with flowers and placed in the centre of the room.

The couple may wear plain clothes for the feast, but one of them must have an athame with which to cut the cake. The merriment continues through the rest of the evening.

THE RITE OF COMPASSION

The rite of compassion is enacted to relieve the sadness and guilt that arises from knowing that you have unknowingly caused friends or family grief. This rite can also be performed during times of hardship to obtain the good favour and the protection of the God and the Goddess.

PREPARATION

On a night during the full moon, the altar may be set up in preparation for a lunar ritual (see the planetary rituals). The altar is adorned with a white cloth with a single white candle upon it. A light, clean, lunar incense must be chosen and branches of willow (a tree sacred to the moon) can be used to adorn the altar or the temple. The traditional ritual bath is taken before the rite and the circle is cast in the traditional manner. An egg is also required for this rite as an offering.

THE RITE

Once all is in readiness, the circle is cast in the usual manner. When the coven is gathered, the Priestess begins the rite by ritually cleansing her hands in a bowl of water containing hyssop. After she has washed her hands, the Priestess inhales the incense and declares her purity:

I have bathed myself and my hands are clean,
I have inhaled the incense and my words are pure.
Through my purification, may all that is evil now depart,

May I stand pure before thee, O God and Goddess!

Taking up her athame the Priestess invokes the God and Goddess:

> **I thy servant full of sighs,**
> **Call upon thee O God and Goddess.**
> **What can I do O Lady?**
> **That thou shalt smile upon me?**
> **Pale Lady of the moon, in my heart I find no ease.**
> **Acceptest thou my offering,**
> **And give unto me a sign that thou art appeased!**

The Priestess then makes either a bloodless offering of incense or she makes a blood offering and breaks an egg. The Priestess continues the invocation:

> **What may I do? O God and Goddess,**
> **That my sins might be absolved?**
> **I behold nothing before me, but misery.**
> **O God and Goddess turn your face towards me,**
> **And smile upon me once more!**

After the invocation, the candle is to be extinguished and the circle dissolved.

THE RITE OF THE NEW MOON

The new moon is considered to be a time of ill luck, but money spells are cast upon the appearance of a new moon - it is the belief that as the moon increases so does wealth. For a spell to increase wealth, take three silver coins, some lunar incense, and a large shell. The altar is set up as for a lunar rite and the circle is to be cast in the usual manner. Upon the night of the new moon, cleanse and consecrate the three silver coins and the shell in the traditional manner. Fill the shell with water, and then turn each of the three coins three times, in the shell, reciting the spell:

Turn my silver three times three, turn the tide of luck to me.

Repeat this every time you turn a coin. When you have finished, dry the coins and toss them from one hand to the other, while repeating the following chant, faster and faster, until you err, then stop:

Who'll have silver? Who'll have gold?
Who'll have the secret? Who'll be told?
I'll have silver, I'll have gold
I'll have the secret, I'll be told!

Once you have finished this, put the coins away safely.

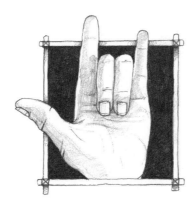

THE RITE OF DRAWING DOWN THE MOON

Wiccans uphold the ancient tradition of performing the nature myths upon the Sabbats, and for these rites the Priestess must play the part of the Goddess. In keeping with the ancient tradition, the Goddess is called down from the Moon and into the body of the High Priestess, the Priestess then becomes the living embodiment of the Goddess for the remainder of the rite. The invoking of the Goddess into the Priestess is called *drawing down the moon*.

The Goddess is also known as Aradia, Brighid, Diana and Artemis. She is the flowers and the fields. She is the moon as the maiden, mother and crone. She is the essence of all that is feminine. She is the rain and the corn. She is the Green Goddess and the White Goddess. She is merciful, beautiful and in her many guises she becomes all things to all men and all women. The Goddess also has a darker side, which is often portrayed as her sister. In her dark guise she is Cerridwen, Hecate, Sheela-na-gig, a Goddess of deep water, destiny, darkness and barren earth. She is a Goddess of dark caves and twisted trees, of sorrow, pain, blood and death.

After the circle has been cast in the normal manner, (see casting the circle) the Priest is to crown the Priestess with a Lunar crown and kneel before her. The Priestess then stands with her arms in the air and her legs together - this is an ancient posture called the crows-foot and it represents the female genitalia. The Priest then begins the rite by giving her 'The fivefold salute':

Blessed are thy feet,
That have brought thee this way.

(The Priest kisses her feet.)

Blessed are thy knees
That shall kneel at the sacred altar.

(The Priest kisses her knees.)

Blessed be thy womb,
Without which we would not be.

(The Priest kisses her abdomen.)

Blessed be thy breasts,
Formed in perfect beauty.

(The Priest kisses her breasts.)

Blessed are thy lips
That shall utter the sacred names.

(The Priest kisses her upon the lips.)

The Priest then makes the sign of the Horned God with his index and little finger (without standing up) and places his fingers on the floor to the earth. The Priest then invokes the Goddess down into the body of the Priestess:

I invoke thee and call upon thee,
Mighty Mother of us all,
Bringer of all fruitfulness,
By seed and root, by bud and stem,
By leaf and flower, and fruit,
I do invoke thee, to descend upon this,
The body of this thy servant and Priestess!

Hail Aradia! Mighty Mother of us all,
From thy Amalthean horn, pour forth thy store of love,
I lowly bend before thee, thy foot is to my lip,
With loving sacrifice thy shrine adorn,
I adore thee to the end.

My prayers rise upon the rising incense smoke.
Then spend thine ancient love O Goddess,
Descend into this, the body of thy Priestess and servant,
Aid me, for without thee, I am forlorn!

The Priest rises and steps back, the Priestess (who is now the Goddess) takes up her athame and draws an invoking pentagram in the air before him:

Of the Mother Darksome and divine,
Mine the scourge, and mine the kiss:
The five-pointed star of love and bliss,
Here I charge thee, with this sign.

The Goddess lays down her athame and stands in the posture of the crow's foot. The rite of Drawing down the moon completed, the Priestess and Priest turn to face the coven. The Priest addresses the coven:

Listen to the words of the Great Mother,
She who of old was also called among men,
Artemis, Astarte, Cerridwen, Bride, and many other names!

The Priestess then says to the coven:

Whenever ye have need of anything,
Once in the month, and better it be,
When the moon is full,
Then shall ye assemble in some secret place,
And adore the spirit of me,
Who am Queen of all witches.

There shall ye assemble, all ye who are fain
To learn all sorcery,
Yet have not won its deepest secrets.
To these will I teach things that are yet unknown,
And ye shall be free from slavery,
And as a sign that ye are really free,
Ye shall be naked in your rites.
And ye shall dance, sing, feast,
Make music, and love, all in my praise.
For mine is the ecstasy of the spirit,
And mine also is joy on earth,
For my law is love unto all beings.

Keep pure your highest ideal; strive ever toward it,
Let naught turn you aside.
For mine is the secret door that opens upon the land of youth,
Mine is the cup of the wine of life,
And mine, the cauldron of Cerridwen,
Which is the grail of immortality.

I am the gracious Goddess,
Who gives the gift of joy unto the heart of every man.
Unto earth, I give the knowledge of the spirit eternal.
Beyond death, I give peace and freedom,
Re-union with those who have gone on before us.
Nor do I demand sacrifice, for behold,
I am the Mother of all living things,
And my love is poured out upon the earth.

The Priest calls:

Listen to the words of the Star Goddess,
She is the dust in whose feet are the hosts of heaven
And whose body encircles the universe.

The Priestess takes up the charge:

I who am the beauty of the green earth,
And the white moon among the stars,
And the mystery of the waters
And the desire in the heart of man, call unto thy soul
Arise, and come unto me for I am the soul of nature,
Who gives life to the universe.
From me all things proceed
And unto me all things must return.
And before my face beloved of Gods and men,
Let thine innermost self be enfolded
In the rapture of the infinite!
Let my worship be within the heart that rejoiceth.
For behold, all acts of love and pleasure are my rites.
And therefore let there be beauty and strength,
Power and compassion, honour and humility
Mirth and reverence within you.
And thou who seekest me,
Know thy seeking and yearning
Shall avail thee not unless thou knowest the mystery;
That if that which thou seekest,

Thou findest not within thee,
Then thou wilt never find it without thee.
For behold, I have been with thee from the beginning,
And I am that which is attained at the end of desire!

The charge complete, the coven rise and the Priest calls:

Bagahi laca bachahe, Lamac cahi achabah Karrelyos,
Lamac lamac bachalyos, Cabahagi sabalyos,
Lagozatha cabyolas, Samahac et famyolas, Harrahya!

The Priestess then invokes the God into the body of the Priest - this
is called Drawing Down the Sun.

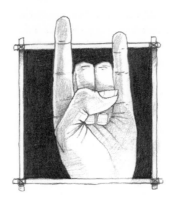

THE RITE OF DRAWING DOWN THE SUN

At the Sabbats, the presence of the Horned God is also required and the spirit of the Horned God is called down into the body of the Priest - as the Goddess is called down into the Priestess. The Horned God is many things, he is Cernunnos, he is the sun and he is the wild places. He is the spirit of the great forests and the wild creatures. He is the dying God of vegetation, the great white stag, the ram, the bull and the essence of all that is masculine. The Horned God also has a darker side that is often spoken of as his brother. In this guise he becomes Herne the hunter, and guide to the underworld. He is also Nudd or Arawn, Lord of Anwyn (the underworld) who emerges by night and prowls with his pack of ravenous hounds. He is the Dark Lord of Time, Chaos and Destiny.

THE RITE

The Priestess places the horned helmet upon the head of the Priest and kneels before him. She then gives the Priest the fivefold salute while he assumes the posture of the Horned God (arms wide but bent at the elbows).

Blessed are thy feet, that have brought thee this way.
(The Priestess kisses his feet.)

Blessed are thy knees, that shall kneel at the sacred altar.
(The Priestess kisses his knees.)

Blessed be thy phallus, without which we would not be.
(The Priestess kisses his abdomen.)

Blessed be thy breasts formed in strength and beauty.
(The Priestess kisses his breasts.)

Blessed are thy lips that shall utter the sacred names.
(The Priestess kisses him upon the lips.)

The Priestess then makes the sign of the Goddess by extending her thumb, forefinger and little finger (without standing up) and places her fingers on the floor. The Priestess then invokes the God down into the body of the Priest:

Depth calls on height, the Goddess calls the God.
He who is the flame that quickens her.
That they both may seize the silver reins
And ride as one the twin-horsed chariot.
Let the hammer strike the anvil.
Let the lightning strike the earth.
Let the lance find the grail.
Let magic come to birth!
In the name of the Goddess do I invoke thee,
O Horned God, the mighty father of us all,
Lugh, Pan, Bel, Herne, Cernunnos.
Great God Herne, come in answer to my call,
And show yourself to men once more,
Descend I pray thee, into thy servant and Priest!

The Priest then takes up his athame and draws the invoking pentagram in the air before the Priestess. The Priestess rises and the Priest stands in the posture of the Horned God (arms wide, legs apart).

The Horned God is once more among us!

The rite of the drawing down of the sun is ended.

COUNTER SPELLS

To return the spell of another, images and magic mirrors are employed. Sometimes the spell is returned to the sender using the mirror or an image along with a suitable incantation; sometimes cords are employed with spells of '*binding*'. Binding spells are incantations of restriction that are intended to cause no harm but restrict the movements of the recipient of the spell.

BURNING THE IMAGE

One method of repelling a magical attack is to burn an image of the attacker with a counterspell. The circle is cast in the traditional manner and the Priestess makes an image of her attacker. The Priestess then gives life to the image in the traditional manner. Having done this, the Priestess must then select her method of repelling the attack. One way of countering a spell is to utter a counterspell three times, over an image while it burns.

> **Arise Horned God and hear my call!**
> **Grant me thy protection!**
> **O Thou who hast made my image,**
> **I know thee not,**
> **But I shall return thy spell threefold.**
> **May my spell be thy spell, may I suffer not!**
> **Thy image I shall burn, and may my curse, be thy curse!**

After the ritual, the incense and the candle are extinguished.

BINDING SPELLS

To stop gossip and evil deeds the image can be bound with a white thread around the feet, knees, mouth, eyes and hands. On the night of the full moon bind the image and recite the spell.

> **O thou who carries the word**
> **Of my misfortune in thy heart,**
> **Whose tongue would bring about my destruction,**
> **Through whose lips I am poisoned,**
> **In whose footsteps death follows,**
> **I seize thy mouth; I still thy tongue,**
> **I bind thy restless feet,**
> **I close thy piercing eyes,**
> **I bind thy active knees,**
> **I seize thy outstretched hands,**
> **And tie them behind thee!**
> **May the Goddess return thy blow!**
> **May your charms come to naught!**

The image is then kept safe until the mischief stops.

REQUIEM

M odern Witches believe that after their physical bodies die their souls journey to a hidden land where no living mortal can go. The land beyond death is known as the Land of Summer. Here the souls of the dead remain protected until it is time for their rebirth.

When a modern witch dies the funeral service has to be held in a church or a crematorium because Wicca is not a recognized religion. However, in some crematoria the officiating priest is pagan-friendly, and will allow for a slight pagan theme.

When a witch dies, the members of the coven assemble to hold their own remembrance service. During this rite, each person lights a candle to say farewell to the deceased and the High priestess enacts the descent of Ishtar into the Underworld. Those that have passed on to the Summerland are also remembered every year at the Halloween festival. There is a rule that at the Halloween festivals and the requiems no newcomers or outsiders are allowed to take part. However, there is no reason why close friends that are sympathetic to the craft cannot be invited. In the myths the Goddess Ishtar descends to the underworld naked, therefore to make the following rite more suitable for outsiders to take part in, the descent of Ishtar is omitted.

THE RITE

The altar and the temple room are to be adorned with branches of yew, the tree of immortality, and white lilies. On the altar are placed candles for those who are to attend the rite. A cauldron is placed in the centre of the room in which the rite is to be held. For the rite, the Priest and Priestess wear black robes. The circle is cast in the traditional manner before any outsiders arrive and the coven awaits all those who are to take part in the rite.

The Priest places a candle in the cauldron and taking the spare candles from the altar he goes to stand by the door. As each person passes by him the Priest hands them a candle. He then lights a taper from the central candle on the altar and lights the candle in the cauldron with it.

The Priestess calls:

> We gather this night in sadness and in joy
> To say farewell to (name) our beloved friend,
> We are sad for our loss
> Yet content in our knowledge
> That when our time comes, as it surely must,
> We too will journey to the Summerland gladly and unafraid.
> For we know that once rested and refreshed
> Amongst our loved ones, we too shall be reborn
> Through the grace of the Lord and the Lady.
> O God and Goddess,
> Let it be in the same time and place as our loved ones
> And may we meet them and know them,
> And remember them and love them once again.

The Priestess lights her candle from the one in the cauldron and she tells those assembled to do likewise. The Priestess places her candle in the cauldron and says to those gathered:

> Let each of us take a light from the flame
> And place a token of remembrance
> In the cauldron before us,
> For one day we shall want others to do likewise for us.

Those gathered place their candles upright in the cauldron and the Priestess says a few words about the deceased. The Priest does likewise then the Priestess calls:

> Would anyone like to say a few words?

79

Those that wish to say a little about the deceased then do so. The Priestess then calls:

Are there any that would like to make their peace?

At this point of the rite any that have something to say to the deceased do so. The Priestess then calls:

Let us look well into the eternal flame
And let think of our dear one and all those
Whom we have loved and have also passed on!

All those gathered then sit and meditate upon the flames in the cauldron. After a while, a bell is rung softly by the Priest to signal the end of the meditation.

Come! The time to shed tears is over,
Let us make merry and enjoy life,
for they would wish it no other way.
Let us look to the future and celebrate the time
When we shall once more meet our loved ones.

As death follows life so does life follow death
And as one generation passes, the next doth appear,
Only the Goddess remains the same.
Come join me in the feast!

A celebratory feast of farewell ensues.

CHAPTER FIVE

THE INITIATIONS

FIRST-DEGREE INITIATION

First-degree initiation is only offered to guests who have attended coven meetings for over three months. Those that wish to join the coven have to acquire for themselves an athame and a cord. Initiations take place only on the nights of the full moon and never at Sabbats. To begin the initiation ceremony, the circle is cast in the usual manner but the gateway is left open.

The Initiate stands outside the room, blindfolded, with their hands tied loosely behind their back (the ends of the cord are used later, as a halter to lead them into the circle). As the Initiate is bound, the charge is given:

Neither free nor bound!

The Priest then enacts the ritual of Drawing Down the Moon and invokes the Goddess down into the Priestess. The Priestess in turn performs the ritual of Drawing Down the Sun and invokes the God down into the Priest.

The Postulant (Initiate) is then turned around three times to disorientate them and they are turned to face the coven. The Postulant is led towards the circle by the cord. The Initiator greets the Postulant:

Blessed be those within the circle,
Pure of heart and pure of mind,
Where only the truth be spoken
And only the truth be heard.

The Initiator takes up his or her athame and the tip of the athame is pressed against the breast of the Postulant with the charge:

> **O thou who standeth on the threshold,**
> **Do'st thou seek the way?**
> **Wilt thou serve the Goddess**
> **With reverence to the God?**
> **Will thou guard that which is shown thee**
> **And keep it from the unworthy?**
> **For it is better to fall upon my blade and perish**
> **Than make the assay with fear in thy heart!**

The Postulant says: **Aye.**

The blindfold is then removed and the cords are cut. The Initiator whispers unto them:

> **I have two passwords for thee.**
> **Perfect love and perfect trust!**
> **For all who have such are doubly welcome,**
> **I give thee a third with which**
> **To pass through this dread door!**

The Postulant is then spun into the circle with a kiss and the gateway is closed. The Postulant is then introduced to each of the watchtowers in turn:

> **Take heed, ye Lords of the east/south/west/north,**
> **That (name) is properly prepared to be Initiated a witch!**

The Postulant is then led to the centre of the circle where the coven dances around the postulant and the Initiator chanting the witches' rune (see the Witches' Rune, p.37).

The Postulant is then pushed backwards and forwards by the members of the coven to disorient him or her. A bell is then rung three times to signal the end of the jostling and the Initiator addresses the Postulant:

> **In other religions the postulant kneels**
> **Before the Priest and Priestess.**
> **But we of the craft of the wise,**
> **Are taught to be humble,**

And we kneel to welcome thee,
And we say unto thee...

The fivefold salute is then given to the Postulant and the Initiator kisses his or her feet, knees, belly, breasts and lips with the fivefold blessing:

To a female postulant the charge is:

Blessed are thy feet that have brought thee this way.
Blessed are thy knees that shall kneel at the sacred altar.
Blessed be thy womb, without which we would not be.
Blessed be thy breasts, formed in perfect beauty.
Blessed are thy lips that shall utter the sacred names.

To a male postulant the charge is:

Blessed are thy feet that have brought thee this way.
Blessed are thy knees that shall kneel at the sacred altar.
Blessed be thy phallus without which we would not be.
Blessed be thy breasts, formed in perfect strength.
Blessed are thy lips that shall utter the sacred names.

The Postulant is then told:

We are now going to take thy measure!

The Postulant is measured around his or her head, chest, hips, and from the top of the head to the heels. The measure is then placed upon the altar and the Initiator addresses the Postulant:

Thy measure has been taken.
It shall be kept in a secret place known only to me
Under the watchful eyes of the God and Goddess.
Should thou wish to leave the coven at any time
Then thou mayest take thy measure with thee,
And thou mayest go in peace.
But mark thou this,
That the God and Goddess shall bear witness
If thou shouldst ever break thy oath!

The measure may or may not be returned to him or her - this depends on the coven. The Initiator addresses the Postulant again:

Art thou ready to pass the ordeal and be purified?

The Postulant says: **Aye!** and is told to kneel.

A bell is rung three times and the ringer of the bell calls: **"Thrice!"** The Postulant is then given three light strokes with the scourge. At the call of: **"Seven!"** The Postulant is given seven light lashes. At the call of: **"Twenty-one!"** twenty-one lashes are given to the Postulant. The Initiator then addresses the Postulant again:

Thou hast bravely passed the test,
Art thou ready to swear that thou wilt be true to thy art?

The Postulant replies: **I am.**

The Initiator responds with: **Then repeat after me!**

I call upon the God and Goddess,
Mindful that my measure has been taken,
To witness here my oath.
I do solemnly swear of my own free will,
In the presence of the God and Goddess,
That I shall never reveal the Secrets of the craft to any outsider.
I do pledge myself to the coven and to the craft.
I swear to abide by the rules of the coven
And to serve the God and Goddess truly.
In the names of the God and Goddess I do so swear.

The Postulant rises and is then anointed on the belly and both breasts with the holy oil or water. The Initiator says:

I hereby sign thee with the triple sign,
I consecrate thee with oil.

The Postulant is then anointed with wine:

I anoint thee with wine.

The Initiator gives the Postulant a kiss and says:

I consecrate thee with my lips, O witch.
I shall now present thee the tools of the craft!

The Postulant is shown the Sword of Power:

> **First the Sword of Power; with this, as with the athame,**
> **Thou canst form all magic circles,**
> **Dominate, subdue and punish all rebellious spirits**
> **And demons and even persuade angels and good spirits.**
> **With this in thy hand, thou art the ruler of the circle!**

The Initiator gives an athame to the Postulant and says:

> **Next I present thee with the athame; this is thy weapon,**
> **And it has all the powers of the Sword of Power!**

The Postulant is then shown the utility knife:

> **I present the white-handled knife; its use is to form all**
> **Instruments of the art and can only be used in the circle.**

The Postulant is then shown the wand:

> **I present thee the wand.**
> **Its use is to call up and control**
> **Certain angels and genii to whom it**
> **Would not be meet to use the athame!**

The Postulant is then shown the cup:

> **I present thee the cup,**
> **This is the vessel of the Goddess,**
> **It is the cauldron of Cerridwen,**
> **The Holy Grail of immortality**
> **From this we drink in unity and in honour of the Goddess.**

The Postulant is shown the pentacle:

> **I present thee the pentacle for the invoking of the spirits!**

The Postulant is shown the censer:

> **I present thee the censer to encourage**
> **Good spirits and to exorcise evil spirits!**

The Postulant is shown the scourge:

Next I present thee the scourge;
The symbol of power and domination.
It is also used for purification and enlightenment;
For it is written that to learn, you must suffer and be purified.
Art thou willing to suffer to learn?

The Postulant replies: **Aye!**

The Postulant is given the cords:

Lastly, I present thee the cords; they are
To be used to bind the sigils of the art,
Also the material basis;
They are necessary in the oath!

The Postulant is then made welcome:

I salute thee in the name of the God and Goddess.
Welcome O witch, come and join us in the circle.

The Initiate is then introduced to the watchtowers and the athame
and the cords are consecrated. At the end of the rite, the circle is
banished in the usual manner.

SECOND-DEGREE INITIATION

Second degree Initiation can be given only to those who have passed the first-degree initiation and is only given by a third degree High Priest or Priestess. The Priest initiates female witches and the Priestess initiates male ones. At this degree, the witch is given his or her new magical name. To obtain this degree, knowledge of how to use the tools of the craft is required.

The circle is to be cast in the usual manner and the God and Goddess are to be invoked into the body of the Priest and Priestess as it was with the first-degree initiation. When all is in readiness, the Initiator calls to the Initiate:

> **Thou art summoned ‑ Walk with the sun**
> **To the north of the circle and turn to face us!**

The Initiate walks clockwise to the north of the circle and faces the Initiator. The Initiate is then bound, blindfolded and introduced to each of the watchtowers in turn:

> **Take heed, ye Lords of**
> **The eastern/southern/western/northern portal.**
> **That (name) is properly prepared to be initiated**
> **A second‑degree witch!**

The Initiate is then led to the centre of the circle where the coven dances around the Initiate and Initiator chanting the Witch's rune.

The Initiate is then made to kneel before the altar and the Initiator addresses the Initiate:

To attain this degree, it is necessary to suffer and be purified
Art thou willing to suffer to learn?

The Postulant replies: **Aye!**

The Initiator returns with: **I purify thee to take this oath rightly!**

A bell is rung three times and the ringer of the bell calls: "Thrice!" The Postulant is then given three light strokes with the scourge. At the call of: "Seven!" the Postulant is given seven lashes. At the call of: "Twenty-one!" The Postulant receives twenty-one lashes. The Initiator then addresses the Postulant:

I now give thee a new name. What is thy name?

The Initiator gives the Postulant a stroke of the scourge and the Initiate replies:
      My name is _____.

The Initiator asks: **Repeat after me:**

I (name) do solemnly swear of my own free will,
In the presence of the God and Goddess,
That I shall never reveal the secrets of the craft to any,
Save it be to a worthy person, properly prepared,
In the centre of a magic circle such as I am in now.
This I swear by my hopes of salvation, my past lives
And my hopes for my future lives to come.
And I give myself and my measure unto destruction
If I ever break my oath.
I pledge myself to the coven and to the craft.
And I swear to abide by the rules of the coven
And to serve the God and Goddess truly.
In the names of the God and Goddess, I do so swear.

The Initiator kneels and places their left hand on the Postulant's knee and their right hand upon the Postulant's head. The Initiator then gives some of their power to the Initiate:

I will all my power unto thee!

The Initiate is then unbound and helped to rise. The blindfold is then removed. The Initiate is then anointed on the belly, right breast, left hip, right hip, left breast and belly with the holy oil:

**I hereby anoint thee with the sacred pentagram,
I consecrate thee with oil.**

The Postulant is then anointed with wine:

I anoint thee with wine.

The Initiator gives the Postulant a kiss and says to them:

**I consecrate thee with my lips O witch.
Thou shalt now use the tools of the craft!**

The Postulant is given the sword of power:

First the sword of power!

The Postulant recasts the circle with the sword without speaking. The Initiator then gives the Postulant the athame.

Next the athame!

The Postulant casts the circle again without words. The Postulant is then given the utility knife and a candle from the altar:

The white-handled knife.

The Postulant carves a pentagram on the candle. The Postulant is then given the wand with which they salute the watchtowers:

Next the wand!

The Postulant is then handed the cup and the Initiate and Initiator consecrate the vessel in the appropriate manner:

Next the cup!

The Postulant is then handed the pentacle and the postulant salutes the watchtowers with it:

Sixth, the pentacle for the invoking of the spirits!

The Postulant is then handed the censer with which he or she again recasts the circle:

Seventh the censer, to encourage good spirits and expel evil!

The Postulant is then given the cords with which he or she binds their Initiator:

Eighth, the cords!

The Postulant is then given the scourge:

Ninth, the scourge,
For learn in the craft that you must ever give
As you receive, but ever triple.
So where I gave 3 you shall return 9,
Where I gave 9 you shall return 27,
And where I gave 21, you shall return 63!

The numbers are called and the Initiator is given the lashes. The Initiator then says:

Thou hast obeyed the law, but mark well,
When thou receiveth good,
So equally art thou bound to return good threefold!

The Initiator is helped to stand. The Postulant is then introduced to each of the watchtowers in turn.

Ye Lords and guardians of the watchtowers
of the east/south/west/north.
(Name) is duly consecrated a second-degree witch!

THIRD-DEGREE INITIATION

Only a third-degree member can give a third-degree initiation to a second-degree member. A third degree initiation is required to run a coven. The rite is given upon request if the Priest and Priestess regard the candidate as suitable.

To begin this rite, the circle is cast in the usual manner and the Priest and the Priestess invoke the God and the Goddess into each other. Either the Priestess or the Priest depending upon their sex then initiates the Initiate. In this ritual, the Initiate is female and is initiated by the Priest. The ritual for both male and female is much the same, but the roles change over. This ritual is performed sky clad.

The Priest stands in the posture of Osiris arisen, with arms crossed over his chest, and the Priestess kneels before him (if the Initiate is male, the Priestess assumes the Goddess posture). She places her forearms alongside his thighs, and places her forehead upon his knees in salute. After a pause she rises and fetches a wine-filled chalice from the altar and again kneels before him. The Priestess raises the cup to the Priest and the Priest consecrates the wine with his athame. The Priest calls:

As the athame is to the male, so the cup is to the female,
And in their conjoining they bring great blessedness.

The athame is laid down on the altar and the Priestess stands. The Priestess drinks from the cup and passes the cup to the Priest for him to drink from - with a kiss and a blessing. The Priest drinks from the cup and then hands the cup to the Initiate - also with a kiss and a blessing, so that she may drink from the cup. The cup is then handed to the coven so that they may drink. The bread is then brought forth and consecrated in the usual manner (see the ceremony of cakes and wine) and all partake of the bread. The Priest then asks the Initiate:

Ere I dare proceed with this sublime rite,
I must beg purification at thy hands.

The Priest is then bound and led before the altar. The Priest is given three strokes with the scourge and then untied. The Initiate is then given three lashes with the scourge by the Priest and also released. Recognition is then asked from each of the watchtowers in turn:

Take heed, ye Lords of the east / south / west / north,
That ____ is properly prepared
To be initiated as a High Priestess!

The Priest leads the Initiate before the altar and declares:

I beg purification again!

The lashes are repeated and the Priest rises saying:

Now I must reveal a great mystery!

The Initiate adopts the Goddess posture before the altar and the Priest gives her the fivefold blessing. The Initiate then lays in the sacred circle with her head to the east. The Priest kneels between her legs and facing north, the Priest invokes the Goddess into the Initiate with the charge:

Assist me to erect the ancient altar,
At which, in days past, all worshipped,
For in olden times woman was the altar.
Thus was the altar made and placed
And the sacred point was the point
Within the centre of the circle,
As we have of old been taught that the point
Within the centre is the origin of all things,
Therefore we should adore it!

The Priest kisses her abdomen:

> **Therefore whom we adore we also invoke,**
> **By the power of the lifted lance!**

The Priest continues:

> **O circle of stars (Priest kisses Initiate) whereof our father**
> **Is but the younger brother, marvel beyond imagination**
> **Soul of infinite space, before whom time is bewildered**
> **And understanding dark,**
> **Not unto thee may we attain unless thine image be loved.**
> **Therefore by seed and root by bud and stem,**
> **By leaf and flower and fruit, do we invoke thee!**
> **O queen of space, O dew of light,**
> **Continuous one of the heavens,**
> **Let it be ever thus, that men speak not of thee as one**
> **But as none; and let them not speak of thee at all,**
> **Since thou art continuous.**
> **For thou art the point in the circle which we adore**
> **The font of life without which we would not be!**

The Priest kisses the Initiate on the abdomen again.

> **And in this way are erected the holy twin pillars.**

The Priest kisses her left breast, then her right breast:

> **In beauty and in strength were they erected,**
> **To the wonder and glory of all men!**

At this point in the rite, the coven must leave the room or turn their backs. Only the High Priestess is allowed to oversee the Great Rite. The Priest then continues the charge:

> **O secrets of secrets, thou art hidden**
> **In the being of all lives, now thee do we adore.**
> **For thou which adoreth is also thou.**
> **Thou art that, and that am I.**

The Priest kisses her abdomen again:

> **I am the flame that burns in the heart of every man,**
> **And in the core of every star,**
> **I am life and the giver of life.**
> **Yet therefore is the knowledge of me the knowledge of death.**
> **I am alone, the life within ourselves**
> **Whose name is mystery of mysteries.**

The Priest gives the Initiate the fivefold salute again. The Priest then lays upon the Initiate and invokes:

> **May the God and the Goddess**
> **Lift the veil between us.**
> **For these are the five points of fellowship -**
> **Foot to foot, knee to knee, lance to grail,**
> **Breast to breast lips to lips**
> **By the great and holy names of Cernunnos and Aradia,**
> **Encourage our hearts; let the light crystallize itself**
> **In our blood, fulfilling us in resurrection.**
> **For there is no part of us that is not of the Gods!**

The Priest and the new Priestess arise and go to each of the cardinal points in turn and greet the watchtowers:

> **Ye lords and guardians of the watchtowers**
> **Of the east / south / west / north,**
> **The thrice consecrated High Priestess**
> **Greets thee and thanks thee!**

CHAPTER SIX

THE EIGHT SABBATS

The ancient farmers knew how to predict the coming seasons through the changes in their surroundings. By watching the plants and trees and the habits of the animals they knew what season was at hand. The seasons dictate when to plant and when to reap and governed the lives of the ancient agricultural settlements.

The ancient Priests knew how to establish the time of the year through the passage of the sun and the moon. They also knew that the hours of sunlight waxed and waned throughout the year and at certain times of the year, darkness and light stood in balance. The knowledge of the annual changes in sunlight provided the ancients with the ability to fix the times of the seasons. The ancients possessed four calendars; an agricultural calendar, a solar calendar, a quarter day calendar, and a lunar calendar.

The ancient Europeans celebrated four seasonal changes. The flora and fauna dictated these changes. For example, when the Elms opened their leaves, it was time to start sowing seed (Imbolc) and when the Ashes dropped their leaves, winter was on its way. Festivals were also held at the times when night and day stood in perfect balance (the equinoxes), and when the sun was at its lowest and its highest points - the solstices. Wiccans celebrate all eight festivals and they call them the Sabbats (holy days).

THE FIRE FESTIVALS

As one season died and the next began, great fires were lit upon the hillsides. These ancient fires are known as *Bonfires* or *Balfires*. Bonfire is a French term, which means *good fire*, and Balfire is a Babylonian word meaning *fire of the Lord*. Upon these huge fires was burned all the dross from the last season's growth. At these times of year it was customary to celebrate and welcome in the new season. When the agricultural festivals were given fixed dates, the Balfires were lit on the nights before 2nd February, 1st May, 1st August, and 1st November.

On the Fire Festivals, Wiccans enact the nature myths just as they were in ancient times. The nature myths tell the story of the changing seasons. In the myths, the God of Vegetation is missing for the season of destruction because at that time of the year nothing will grow. Although the God of Vegetation "dies" with the harvest, he is in fact immortal, and during the season of destruction he withdraws to the underworld. While the God of Green Growth awaits his rebirth, he becomes the caretaker of all the souls who are with him. Those he judges worthy will be reborn (Wiccans call this land the Summerland).

Meanwhile, the God of Chaos lays waste to the countryside causing death and destruction. The Green Goddess searches for her consort and her wailing and her tears become the autumnal winds and rain. Eventually, the Goddess finds her consort and returns him to his throne. The God of Chaos returns to the underworld and is shackled for yet another year during the seasons of green growth.

In Wicca, the Horned God of Fertility, as the Lord of Spring and Summer, is also called the *Green Man, Oak King, Lord of Life* and the *Green King.* As the God of the wild places and wild animals he also becomes the *Stag of Seven Tines, Cernunnos and Herne.* As the life within the crops he becomes the *Corn King* and the *King of Seven Years.* The Green King's dark twin, the Lord of autumn and winter, is known as *Gwynn-ap-Nudd, Lord of the Mound, Arawn, Lord of the Underworld* and the *Holly King.*

In Wicca, the Goddess is portrayed as both mother and bride. As the Goddess of Fertility, she is called Queen *of the May, Briid* and *The Lady.* As the Goddess of the Moon, she is known as *Aradia, Arianrhod, The White Goddess, Diana, Artemis, Hecate,* and *The Pale Lady.* The Green Goddess also has a dark twin sister who is the autumn and the winter. The Dark Goddess resides in the underworld and never leaves her realm. The Dark Goddess is known as *Sheela-na-gig, The Dark Lady, Cerridwen,* and *The Crone.* The Dark Goddess not only represents the barren earth, but also deep, dark, water and the dark phase of the moon. The Dark Goddess is always portrayed as an aging crone whose head is covered by a shawl.

The Oak King and the Holly King, although separate, are two sides of one God. One side of the God is warm and benevolent; the other side of the God is cruel, cold and malevolent. The Horned God personifies the masculine, as does the sun. This is why Herne is also regarded as a Sun God. Through his association with the sun, Herne also becomes a God of Fire. While residing in the underworld, Herne also becomes a God of Judgement.

The Green Goddess and the Dark Goddess although separate, are two sides of one Goddess. One side of the Goddess is passive, generous and gentle, the other side of the Goddess is impassive and destructive. The Green Goddess personifies the feminine, as does the moon. This is why the Green Goddess is also regarded as the Goddess of the Moon. Through her association with the moon (which rules the tides) the Goddess also becomes Goddess of Water.

THE FESTIVALS OF LIGHT

The solar festivals mark important changes in the duration of sunlight. The festivals of light are celebrated upon the summer solstice - which marks the longest day and the shortest night, and the winter solstice - which marks the shortest day and the longest night. The spring equinox and the autumn equinox are the times when light and darkness stand in perfect balance, but after three days, the balance of power shifts. As the spring equinox passes, and the hours of daylight begin to exceed the hours of darkness, so the God of Sunlight defeats his dark twin in battle and reclaims his throne for the summer months. As the autumn equinox passes, it is the God of Darkness who is victorious and he then rules for the winter months. Upon the summer solstice, which is the longest day, the God and the Goddess of the earth are believed to mate and their conjoining is believed to cause the fruit to form on the bough. At the winter solstice the sun begins to rise again and the Sun God is reborn as the Child of Promise.

THE WICCAN YEAR

Feb. 2nd   Imbolc
The Corn God stirs within the earth.

Mar. 21st   Ostara
The Sun God defeats his dark twin.

May 1st   Beltane
The Oak King claims his mate, the May Queen.

June 21st   Litha
The Holly King defeats the Oak King.

Aug. 1st   Lughnasad
The life of the Corn God is taken.

Sept. 21st   Mabon
The Dark God defeats the Sun God.

Nov. 1st   Samhain
The Goddess mourns the Oak King.

Dec. 21st   Yule
The Oak King defeats the Holly King.

The Wiccan year begins on February 2nd which is the first day of spring and the agricultural year (not the solar year). Winter is finally over, but the weather is still cold. The sun is climbing higher in the sky and the ground begins to thaw. The fields can now be ploughed in readiness for the seeds of the future crops. Imbolc (or Candlemass) is the first Fire Festival of the Wiccan year and is celebrated on the evening of February 1st.

The second festival of the Wiccan year is a solar festival and is held on the spring equinox - between March 21st and March 23rd. This is the festival of Ostara or Easter and at this time of the year, night and day stand in balance. When the balance begins to tilt in favour of the sun, the child of promise (sun born at midwinter) is able to defeat his dark twin in battle. The times of warmth can once more return.

The third festival of the Wiccan year is a Fire Festival and is held on the eve prior to May 1st. This is the festival of Beltane or Mayday, and it heralds the beginning of summer. Beltane is the birthday of the young Green God of spring. At this time of the year, the corn is growing strongly.

The fourth festival of the Wiccan year is a solar festival and is held between June 21st and 23rd. This is the festival of Litha or midsummer and it is the time of the great conjunction. At this time of the year, the May Queen mates with the Green God and their conjoining produces the fruit on the bough.

The fifth festival of the year is a Fire Festival and is held on the eve prior to August 1st. This the festival of Lughnasad (or Lammas) and it heralds the beginning of autumn. Lughnasad is a time of joy but also sorrow. For the beginning of the harvest time signals the end of the life of the Green God who resides in the corn.

The sixth festival of the Wiccan year is a solar festival and is held between September 21st and 23rd. This is the festival of Mabon or harvest home and it heralds the fruit harvesting and the autumnal equinox. At this time of the year, Goronwy the God of Darkness is able to defeat his weakening brother and reclaim his throne. From here on, the days grow shorter towards midwinter.

The seventh festival of the Wiccan year is another Fire Festival and is held on the eve prior to November 1st. This is the festival of Samhain or All-souls and it is the last Fire Festival of the year. Samhain heralds the beginning of winter and at this time of year the Green God and the ancestor spirits are mourned.

The eighth and final festival of the Wiccan year is a solar festival and is celebrated between December 21st and 23rd. This is the festival of Yule (the child) otherwise known as the winter solstice. After the winter solstice, the sun begins to rise once more and heralds the return of the Sun God as the Child of Promise.

IMBOLC
(CANDLEMAS)

The Pagan festival of Imbolc - which means in the belly, is held on the eve of February 2nd. Imbolc is also known as the Christian Festival of Candlemas (many lights). Imbolc is the first Fire-Festival of the year and it is celebrated to mark the end of winter and the beginning of spring. At this time of the year, the snowdrops are beginning to appear in the woods heralding the return of the Oak King. At this time of the year, the fields are ploughed and the seeds are sown for the autumn crops.

This time of the year was, in times past, a time of great joy, for those who had survived the cold winter would live to see yet another year. It is traditional in pagan cultures for the Great Rite to be enacted at this time of the year (see Initiation - 3rd degree) because it is the time for the sowing of seed. For this ritual, the High Priestess as the Goddess of spring wears a crown of many lights or a flower tiara. Both represent her youthfulness. Some Wiccans plant wheat seeds at this time of the year in a pot of earth. Others prefer to symbolically lay the phallic wand in Briids bed. Both are symbolic of the conjoining of the God and Goddess but I find the planting of the wheat seed is more meaningful.

The altar is erected in the traditional manner and the room is garlanded with birch twigs - this is the tree associated with renewal and the beginning of the year - or any blossoming tree. Any incense that is burned must be of an earthy nature. For this rite, a small crib made of straw must be made and in it placed a female doll, (this is called Brighid's bed). Some salt, fresh seed, a pot of earth, a pitcher of water, and a broom is also needed. A candle must also be placed inside the cauldron to represent the Balfire.

THE RITE

To begin the rite, the Priest contacts the altar and lights the central candle. The Priest summons the Priestess who enters the room with the members of the coven and contacts the altar (as it is done in the normal circle working). The coven then gathers around the cauldron and the Priestess lights the candle inside it.

After a moment's silence, the candle in the cauldron is extinguished. The room is now in partial darkness and the coven falls silent. The Priestess then addresses the coven and explains to them the nature of the rite:

> Witches all, we gather this night in darkness,
> To celebrate once more the return of spring.
> Within this season, the seed of the Horned God is
> Deeply implanted within the womb of his mother.
> She who is called Brighid!

> The child of the Great Mother
> Is the unborn child of spring,
> Who, hidden away in her womb,
> Moves ever slowly towards the light..

> Soon, the child within the womb shall quicken
> And it shall be time for him to spring forth,
> Once more renewed and refreshed!

> Now is the season for planting
> And the Horned One shall once more return to us
> Through the planting of his seed,
> So that joy of life and love shall once more be ours.

> As winter becomes spring,
> So darkness becomes light.
> Once more we shall know times of warmth and joy.
> But before the sacred fire can be lit,
> The ashes of the past must be swept away.

The coven bows and while they look downward, a young maiden wearing a flower garland sweeps the circle's edge with the broom. The Priestess then rises and while she sprinkles a little salt around the circle's edge she recites the charge for the purification of the ground:

As our ancestors did before us,
Sow a little salt on their place of worship
- So shall we do likewise!

The Priest relights the candle in the cauldron. The Priestess proclaims:

Thus we banish winter,
Thus we welcome spring.
Say farewell to what is dead,
And greet each living thing!

The circle is then cast in the usual manner. The Priest then goes to the altar and takes up the phallic wand, which he raises vertically above his head. The Priestess kneels before the Priest and invokes the spirit of the Horned God down into him (see drawing down the Moon):

Dread Lord of Death and resurrection.
Lord of life and giver of life, The Lord within ourselves,
Whose name is mystery of mystery,
Gladden our hearts and give us thy light,
For there is no part of us that is not of you.
Descend to us we pray thee, upon thy servant and Priest.

The Priestess makes the invoking pentagram over the Priest and the Priest begins to walk deosil around the circle. The Priest takes the hand of the Priestess and the spiral dance towards the centre of the circle begins - the spiral dance is believed to encourage the sun to return.

The Priestess in turn takes hold of the hand of a male, who in turn, after one circuit of the circle, takes hold of the hand of a female. This continues until the entire coven is joining in the dance. While they dance, the Priestess begins the chant:

Enter I the circle, old,
With heart of love and courage bold,
O God and Goddess, hear our call,
Guardians of us, Witches all.
Take our tokens, take our love
Given ye, what else to prove?
As the mill, around we tread,
Fearing nought that lies ahead.

Forge our spirits, keen and bright
And lead us all towards the light.
Spell and symbol, thought and deed,
Are prompted by the Wiccan rede.
Green the Goddess; green the God.
Thee, we praise in thy flaming rod.

At the call of **"Down!"** from the Priestess, the wheel dance stops and the coven sit. After a short rest, the coven returns to their places. The Priestess goes to the altar and facing toward the northern gateway, she calls the Goddess Brighid - who personifies the Green Goddess as a young maiden:

Come Briid and be among us!

The Priestess then calls:

Briid has come! Briid is welcome!

Two maidens are dispatched to fetch Brighid's bed. The maidens return carrying Brighid's bed, which they place in the centre of the circle. The three women that have previously been chosen to represent the three faces of the Goddess (maiden, mother, and crone) go to stand together in the centre of the circle. The Priestess - who portrays the crone, places a shawl over her head and addresses the coven:

**Let us cast behind us the dark robe of winter,
And step once more toward the light.
Now is the time for rebirth, now is the time for joy,
Now is the time for the planting of seed!**

The Priestess holds aloft the bag of seed and the Priest raises the phallic wand above his head. The Priest calls aloud:

> **By the power of the raised wand**
> **Doth the seed find the furrow.**
> **Blessed be the wand.**

A maiden brings a pot of earth before the Priestess and the Priestess calls:

> **The rites of spring belong to all.**
> **To us and all the Gods!**
> **For this is a joyous time, a time for planting.**
> **Blessed be the seed!**

The Priest inserts the wand into the pot of earth, and the Priestess sows the seeds with the charge:

> **I plant this seed in the womb of the Earth Mother,**
> **That it may grow strong and tall,**
> **Nurtured by the milk of the Goddess,**
> **May it be under the protection of the Horned God,**
> **For the corn is life and part of us.**
> **Blessed be the seed.**

A vessel containing water is then brought forth. The Priestess sprinkles some of the water onto the seeds with the charge:

> **With the waters of life, I do bless this seed**
> **For without which we would not be.**

The Priestess then kneels and breathes three times upon the seed:

> **As life was breathed into us,**
> **So shall we breathe life into thee.**
> **In the name of the Great Mother**
> **So mote it be!**

The pot of earth, the water and the wand are then put down on the altar and the phallic wand is placed in the bed alongside the corn doll (this represents the God and the Goddess together in the bridal bed). The ceremony of cakes and wine then follows; after which, the Priestess declares:

Let the feast begin!

The feast then ensues. Seasonal games are also played during and after the feast.

One of the traditional games at this time of the year is the candle game. In this game, the men sit in a circle facing inwards with a lit candle, which they pass around the circle clockwise. The women stand in a circle behind the men, and it is the women's task to lean over and blow out the candle without stepping forward. If a woman manages to do this, she can then give the man responsible for letting her blow it out a couple of whacks with a light stick. He then has to do a forfeit of her choice.

OSTARA
(SPRING EQUINOX)

Ostara is celebrated from March 21st to 23rd and is the first of the festivals of light. Ostara is also known as Eoster, which is the Christian festival of Easter. At this time of year, the giving of painted eggs is traditional; these eggs represent fertility and the protection of the womb. In the agricultural pagan year, the spring equinox sees the end of the seed planting that had begun at Imbolc. In some of the fields the corn is already beginning to sprout.

The Festival of Ostara is a solar festival and is held to mark the time of year when the hours of daylight begin to outnumber the hours of darkness. The child of promise is now strong enough to oppose his darker twin, and emerges from hiding. At this time of year, light and darkness stand in perfect balance, but as Llew, the God of Sunlight, grows steadily stronger he is able to defeat his dark brother Goronwy by piercing him with his sunlight spear. Llew is then able to claim the throne of Goronwy who gradually retreats. The enthroning of Llew heralds the return once more of warmth and sunlight to the land.

For this rite, Gorse - a shrub of hope, or any other spring flower in bloom, is required. A phallic wand, 2 swords or spears and a solar disc are also needed.

THE RITE
The circle is cast in the traditional manner and the Priestess begins the rite with an explanation of the festival:

Witches all, we gather this night,
On the spring equinox,
When night and day stand in perfect balance;
Slowly, the powers of light increase,
And the Sun God, shall win a victory
Over his twin, the Dark Lord,
And in a mighty battle,
He shall pierce him with his sunlight spear!

The Priestess takes up the phallic wand (this can also be a spear) and goes to stand in the west. The Priest goes to stand in the east, and the Priest and Priestess turn to face one another. The Priestess raises the phallic wand (or spear) high and walks slowly deosil to where the Priest stands. Facing the Priest, the Priestess calls:

O thou sun, art thou ready to conquer the Dark Lord
Who is thy twin brother and reclaim thy throne!

The High Priest takes the wand from the Priestess and raises it above his head, he then places the wand upright upon the altar. A maiden lights a taper from the central candle and presents it to the Priest. The Priest then lights the candle in the cauldron while the Priestess makes the invocation:

We light this fire today,
In the presence of the old ones
Without malice, jealousy or envy,
To welcome once more the God of Light.
For we fear nought beneath the sun,
But the Gods themselves.
Thee we invoke, O Lord of Life,
Be thou a bright flame before us.
Kindle within our hearts a love for our fellow man.

The Priest extinguishes the taper and fetches the cords from the altar. The Priestess positions the coven around the edge of the circle and each member takes the end of a cord - the cords are joined together by a knot in the middle. The coven then begins to rotate in the wheel dance using the cords as the spokes of a wheel.

The witch's rune is then chanted until the call of **"down!"** The cords are then placed on the altar and the Priest invokes the Goddess down into the Priestess. The Priestess as the embodiment of the Goddess calls aloud:

Where is he that impersonates the Dark Lord?

The man who impersonates the Dark God steps forward and the Priestess calls:

Thou art the Dark Lord!
God of the Waning year!
Maiden - bring his crown!

The Priestess crowns him and hands him his sword. The Dark Lord is then placed in the centre of the circle. The Priestess calls:

Where is he that impersonates the Sun God?

The person who has been chosen to represent the Sun God then steps forward. The Sun God is not given a weapon. The Priestess addresses him:

Thou art the Sun God!
God of the Waxing year!

The Priestess then places them both in the centre of the circle and asks them to face one another. The Priestess turns to face the coven and declares:

Now, with the warmth of spring arriving,
The reign of the Dark Lord has finally ended.
The God of the Sun has once more
Returned to reclaim his throne.
But for this to happen the Sun God must
Once again slay his darker brother!

The Sun God addresses his darker brother:

Thou hast had thy time of dominion,
Wilt thou stand before the Sun God whom I represent?
The Dark God Goronwy replies:

I cannot, for as light must yield to darkness,
Darkness must yield to light,
And thou must have thy time of dominion.

The Dark Lord hands his brother Llew his weapon saying:

To thee with love, do I yield my reign!

The Dark Lord sinks to the floor and the Priestess covers him with a veil. The Priestess addresses the coven:

The Dark Lord is gone, but with the return
Of autumn, he shall once more
Return to claim his dark throne
Upon the waning of the summer!

The Dark Lord is then led blindfold to a corner of the room. The Sun God is crowned victorious. The Priestess calls:

For six months of the year,
Shalt thou have dominion.
I crown thee, the Sun God!

The Priestess then calls for the coven to join the feast. During the feast, traditional games are played. At the end of the evening the circle is dissolved. It is customary at this time of the year to give painted eggs to the women.

BELTANE
(MAY EVE)

The Fire Festival of Beltane is celebrated on the eve before May 1st. It is the tradition at this time of the year to erect a Maypole. A Maypole is the trunk of a tall, straight tree, such as a birch or a pine. The Maypole is a representation of the phallus of the Horned God of Fertility whose spirit is within the tree. The Maypole is believed to impart the gift of fertility upon all that touch it.

Beltane is the time of the year awarded to the Green God who is also the Oak King and the Horned God. The young Green God is steadily growing stronger as is the Sun God as the summer solstice approaches. At this time of year the herds are returning and among them, the Horned God. The beginning of summer also heralds the rutting season and for this reason summer is called passion time.

For this ritual, the cauldron is again placed in the centre of the circle and a candle is placed inside it (the candle represents the Belfire). May blossom i.e., blackthorn and hawthorn, should be used to decorate the room and a Maypole may be erected outside. A horned helmet, a green scarf and some flower garlands are needed for this rite.

The circle is cast in the traditional manner and the Priestess begins the rite with an address to the coven:

Witches all, we gather once more,
To worship the God and Goddess,

> Hidden from the world are they.
> Thus, hidden away from the sight of others
> Shall we also work the secrets of our craft.
> Tonight is a night of joy,
> For we celebrate the return of summer.
> The May bride awaits the Horned God,
> And tonight from their conjunction
> There shall come great blessedness.
> Let the green woods sing their song,
> For their spirit is strong within us.

The Priest performs the ritual of 'drawing down the moon'. Once this has been done, the Priest crowns the Priestess with a garland of flowers. The Priest says unto her:

> I crown thee, Queen of the May.

The Priestess (as the Goddess) addresses the coven:

> I am the Lady who impersonates the Goddess of spring.
> As the power of the Goddess is within this season planted,
> So is the power of the Horned God,
> And to him must ye give worship also.

The Priest lays down on the floor in front of the Priestess and she covers him with a green scarf. The Priestess after a minute silence calls:

> The Oak King is dead.
> He has embraced the Great Mother
> And died from his love.
> So has it been year after year.
> Yet if the Oak King is dead,
> All is dead.
> The fields bear no crops.
> The trees bear no fruit.
> The creatures of the Great Mother bear no young.
> What shall we do then?
> That the Oak King shall return?

The coven call:

> Rekindle the Belfire!

The Priestess calls:

So Mote it be!

The Priestess lights a taper from the central candle and lights the candle in the cauldron. The Priestess tells the coven:

Takest thou each a taper and rekindle the Belfire!

Each person goes to the altar and taking up a taper, they light it from the central candle. The tapers are placed in the cauldron. The Priestess calls upon the Oak King to return:

O Thou who art the Oak King,
Return to us once more
That the land may once again be fruitful!

The scarf (shroud) is removed from the body of the High Priest and he rises slowly to his feet. Once he is standing erect he faces the Priestess and says unto her:

I come my lady in answer to your call!

The Priestess crowns him with the horned helmet and says unto him:

Greetings to thee, thou who art the Oak King!

The Priestess and Priest kiss and the Priest replies:

I do thank thee, and in my duties
Shall I ever give homage to thee!

The Priestess calls:

O thou of the joyous craft,
The Oak King has returned.
I decree that thou shalt dance,
That we may be free from the seasons of storms,
As I do dance, so shalt thou follow.
So mote it be!

The Priestess takes the hand of the Priest and leads the coven in the spiral dance. When all are dancing, the procession moves slowly clockwise towards the centre of the room - in imitation of the passage of the sun. After the dance, the ceremony of the bread and wine is performed. The Priestess calls to the Priest:

> I call thee, O thou who impersonates the God,
> To join me in the love-chase,
> For when the Goddess calls,
> There are none who would not willingly go,
> For her libation must be made with
> Love and pain in the magical chase!

The Priest then chases the elusive Priestess with the green scarf until eventually at the end of the song he catches her. During the love-chase, the men sit in the south of the circle and the women sit in the north of the circle. They each in turn sing a verse of the Oak King's song:

THE OAK KING'S SONG

Chorus:

> Cunning and art he did not lack
> But I her whistle, would fetch him back.

Men:

> O I shall go into a hare, with sorrow, sighing and michel care,
> That I shall go into the hall, in the great Gods name,
> Ere that I be fetched thee haim.

Women:

> Hare take heed of the bitch greyhound
> Who'll harry thee close, these fells around
> For here I come in my lady's name
> All but for to fetch thee haim.

Chorus:

> Cunning and art he did not lack
> But I her whistle, would fetch him back.

Men:

> O I shall go into a trout, with sorrow,
> sighing and michel care,
> And strow thee many a crooked game,
> Ere that I be fetched thee haim.

Women:

Trout take heed of an otter lank,
Who'll harry thee close
From bank to bank.
For here I come in my lady's name
All but for to fetch thee haim.

Chorus:

Cunning and art he did not lack,
But I her whistle, would fetch him back.

Men:

O I shall go into a bee, with michel horror and dread of thee!
And inflict a hive in the Horned Gods' name,
Ere that I be fetched thee haim.

Women:

Bee take heed of a swallow hen
Who'll harry thee close, both bat and hen
For here I come in my lady's name
All but for to fetch thee haim.

Chorus:

Cunning and art he did not lack,
But I her whistle, would fetch him back,

Men:

O I shall go into a mouse,
And haste me unto the miller's house
And there in his corn, have good game
Ere that I be fetched thee haim.

Women:

Mouse take heed of a white tid cat
That never was fraught of mice nor rat,
For I'll crack thy bones in my lady's name
All but for to fetch thee haim.

Chorus:

Cunning and art he did not lack,
But I her whistle would fetch him back.

At the end of the song, the Priest finally catches the Priestess. The Priest kisses her, and they enact the Great Rite symbolically. The Priest then hands the scarf to the next man who then chases his partner or a woman of his choice. The love-chase then continues until all the members of the coven have joined in the chase. The Priestess calls for the feast to begin. After the feast is over, the circle is closed in the usual manner.

It is customary at this time of the year for the young men of the villages to compete in tasks of strength, cunning and stamina, for the crown of the Horned God. While the men compete, the women make garlands for their hair. The competition lasts until there is a winner who is then crowned the Horned God. Garlands are then placed in the centre of the circle, and the Horned God must choose a garland of his choice. The woman to whom the garland belongs, is then crowned the Queen of May and she becomes the bride of the Horned God. The Maypole dance then follows to lively music and the King and the Queen are tied to the Maypole by the streamers that hang from it. After a time, the streamers are unplatted and they are freed to enact the great rite.

At the end of this rite, it is the custom for the revelers to wander off together into the woods.

LITHA
(MIDSUMMER'S EVE)

The festival of the midsummer solstice falls between June 21st and 23rd. This festival is called Litha, the festival of stones.

The midsummer solstice is one of the festivals of light and marks the longest day of the year. At this time of the year, Llew, the Sun God, and the Oak King are at the height of their power. Midsummer is hailed as the eve of all magic and it is the time of year when the conjoining of the God and the Goddess is thought to bring forth the fruit on the boughs.

For this ritual, the cauldron is placed in the centre of the circle and a candle placed in it to represent the Sun. Summer flowers should be used to decorate the room and the cauldron. A chalice of water and a phallic wand are also required.

THE RITE

The circle is cast in the usual way and the Priestess begins the rite with an explanation of the festival:

> **Witches all, once more we gather**
> **In the midst of summer,**
> **To celebrate in magical rite**
> **The joining of the God and Goddess,**
> **And from their conjoining**
> **Shall come great blessings to us all!**

Tonight is the eve of all magic,
And the fairy folk are abroad.
'Tis time for the blessing,
And the fruit forms on the bough.

The Priest then invokes the Goddess into the body of the Priestess
and addresses the Goddess:

O laughing queen, beautiful and serene,
She who can tame the savage breast,
In thy guise all men come unto thee,
Be with us now, on the eve of all magic!

The Priestess (as the Goddess) addresses the coven:

I am the Lady who represents the Goddess.
As the power of the Goddess is within this season planted,
So is the power of the Horned God,
And to him must ye give worship also.

The witch's rune is then chanted until the call of **"down!"**

The Priestess as the embodiment of the Goddess calls aloud:

Where is he that impersonates the Holly King?

The man who impersonates the Holly King steps forward and the
Priestess addresses him:

Thou art the Holly King!
God of the Waning year!
Maiden - bring his crown!

The Priestess crowns him. The Holly King is then placed in the centre
of the circle. The Priestess calls:

Where is he that impersonates the Oak King?

The person who has been chosen to represent the Oak King then
steps forward. The Priestess addresses him:

Thou art the Oak King!
God of the Waxing year!

The Priestess then places them both in the centre of the circle and asks them to face one another. The Priestess turns to face the coven and declares:

> With the Sun God at the height of his power,
> The waxing of the year is accomplished.

> The reign of the Oak King is over
> And the waning of the year begins.

> The Holly King must slay his brother the Oak King
> And rule over the land until the depth of winter.
> When his brother shall be born again.

The two Gods grip each other by the shoulders and a struggle takes place. Eventually the Holly King forces the Oak King onto his knees. The Priestess then blindfolds the Oak King and dances around him. While the Priestess dances, the Priest sings the song:

> Dance Lady dance, on the Oak King's tomb,
> Where he lies half a year in the earth's quiet womb.
> Dance Lady dance, at the Holly King's birth,
> Who has slain his brother for his love of earth.

> Dance Lady dance, to the Sun God's power,
> And his golden touch on field and flower.
> Dance Lady dance, with thy blade in hand,
> Summon the sun to bless the land.

> Dance Lady dance, in the silver wheel,
> Where the Oak King rests, his wounds to heal.
> Dance Lady dance, for the Holly King's reign,
> 'Til his brother the Oak King shall rise again.

> Dance Lady dance, in the moonlit sky,
> To the threefold name men know thee by.
> Dance Lady dance, on the turning earth,
> For the birth that is death and the death that is birth.

> Dance Lady dance, for the sun on high,
> For his burning splendour, too, must die.
> Dance Lady dance, for the year's long tide,
> For through all change thou must abide.

Dance Lady dance, for the sun in glory,
Dance Lady dance, to the unending story!

The Oak King is then led blindfold to a corner of the room. The Priestess addresses the coven:

The spirit of the Oak King has gone from us,
To rest in the castle of the silver wheel,
Until with the turning of the year, the season shall come
When he shall return again to rule.

The spirit is gone, therefore,
Let the man that stood for that spirit be freed also.

The High Priestess calls:

Let the Midsummer fires shine forth!

The Holly King then lights the candle in the cauldron. The Priest takes up the phallic wand and the Priestess takes up a chalice of water. The Priestess kneels before the Priest and she holds up the chalice. The Priest plunges the phallic wand in the chalice and the Priestess calls:

Lance to grail, spirit to flesh,
Man to woman, sun to earth.

The coven kneel and the Priestess takes the chalice around the circle anointing each person with the water in the chalice. As the Priestess does this, the Priest calls:

By the waters of the Goddess be ye blessed,
As is the sun when he ariseth in his strength
In the sign of the waters of life!

The chalice is put back on the altar and the Priestess calls:

I decree that thou shalt dance.

The Priest leads the spiral dance while the Priestess calls:

As one generation doth pass and the next appear,
So has thy people always continued.

> And as one season doth pass and the next appear,
> Thou hast returned to us O Lord and Lady.
> So that joy of love and life and warmth,
> Shall once more be ours.

The Priestess calls for the feast to begin. After the feast is over, the circle is closed in the usual manner.

LUGHNASAD
(HARVEST HOME)

The Fire Festival of Lughnasad is celebrated upon the eve before August 1st. Lughnasad marks the transition of summer into autumn and heralds the beginning of the time of harvesting. It was the belief that the spirit of the Horned God/Green King resided in the corn and with the harvest, the life of the King was taken. In times past, the role of the Horned God was awarded to the winner of the Mayday games. The winner of the games would then assume the mantle of the Horned God as the Green King for seven years. During this time, should the crops fail, he was expected to forfeit his life in return for the honours that had been bestowed upon him during his reign. It was the belief that the departure of his spirit into the soil would ensure the return of fertility to the land.

The King of seven years was regarded as the living embodiment of the Horned God and after his death, a little of his blood was used to bless the people - so they could share in his divinity (some was possibly added to the bread and wine). Before the sacrificial King was slain, however, he was allowed to conjoin with any women who chose to mate with him so that his life would continue. This ancient festival is still celebrated in salute to the memory of "He who gave his life willingly so that others might live on." Those who are left behind do not mourn long, because it is believed that death leads to rebirth. This time of year is a time of sadness and joy, sacrifice and love.

The following ritual has been amended because of the confusion between the festivals of Lughnasad and Mabon. Lughnasad is an agricultural festival and Mabon a festival of light.

THE RITE

For this rite, the room and the cauldron should be adorned with oak leaves. A candle is placed in the cauldron to represent the Balfire and the pot of earth from Imbolc, showing ripe corn, is placed on the altar. The circle is cast in the traditional manner.

The Goddess is invoked into the body of the Priestess and the God is invoked into the body of the Priest. The Priestess covers her head with her shawl (in this guise she becomes the Dark Goddess). The Priestess proclaims aloud the intention of the rite:

> **Witches all, the Goddess is kind when it pleases her,**
> **But she who is the day is also the night,**
> **And at times she dost require blood,**
> **Strife and darkness for her purpose.**
> **At this time of the year in times past,**
> **It was the custom for the King who ruled**
> **To be sacrificed in a solemn rite,**
> **So that famine, storm and war,**
> **Should not afflict the people.**
> **And that the crops would grow tall, free from blight.**
> **Darkness would be removed from men's souls**
> **By the courage of one who very willingly**
> **Walked steadily to his doom**
> **So that others would live on.**
> **We gather this night in darkness,**
> **To enact in symbolical dance and magical rite,**
> **The rite of the Green King's sacrifice**
> **As it was done in ages past.**
> **For in this day, our lady no longer**
> **Requires sacrifice of any among us,**
> **For the life she gives is sweet.**

The Priestess calls upon the Priest to come forth:

> **Where is he that impersonates the Horned God?**

At her request, the Priest steps forward and kneels before her. The Priestess anoints him in the sign of the pentagram (see the fivefold blessing) and calls:

I crown thee, the Horned God – maiden, bring his crown!

The Priestess crowns the Priest and addresses him as the Horned God:

Thou who art the Horned God
Art also the life within the Corn!

The Priest replies:

O laughing Queen, beautiful yet terrible,
Thou who like all women can make and destroy men.
Thou art beyond all blame for thou art the Goddess.
As thy sacred blade doth have two edges,
So doth thou possess two faces also.
One is serene, lovely and clear, as thy silver moon.
The other is dark, awesome and cruel,
For thou art likened unto all women.

The Priest hands the Priestess his sword and continues:

Thou who art above all adored,
Know that thy worshippers do give thee obeisance.
The wise, the strong, the powerful,
The very princes of the world do give honour to thee.
The Goddess is kind when it pleases her,
But thou who art the day, art also the night,
And at times thou dost require blood and darkness
For thy dark purpose!

The Priestess addresses the Priest:

Soon the darkness shall be upon us,
And the life of the Corn King must end.
Knowest thou, that in thy sacrifice, thy people shall live on.
Tell me, dost thou still wish to tread the
Path of the Kings before thee?

The Priest answers: **Aye!**

The Priest kneels before the Priestess and the Priestess lifts him up. The Priestess says unto him:

> I do thank thee, but I ask of thee
> One last gift before ye depart.
> Lightest thou the Balfire so that
> Joy of life and love once more be ours!

The Priest lights the candle in the cauldron and returns to the Priestess. The Priestess places the green scarf over his head and they embrace one last time. The Priest chases the Priestess with the scarf until he eventually catches her, then the Priestess chases him. The Priest then attempts to escape and the Priestess pursues him with the green scarf. The rite then takes a sombre turn as the joviality fades and the Priestess pursues him with murderous intent. Eventually the Priestess catches the Priest (who allows himself to be caught). The Priestess addresses him:

> Thou hast had thy time of dominion,
> Wilt thou stand before the Dark Goddess
> Whom I represent?

The Priest replies:

> I cannot, for it is so ordained,
> As winter becomes summer,
> So must summer become winter.
> Life must yield to death, for life to be reborn,
> To thee with love do I yield my reign.

The Priest sinks to the floor and is covered with the green scarf. The Priestess calls aloud:

> The spirit of the God has gone from us,
> To rest in the Summerland,
> Until with the turning of the year,
> The season shall come
> When he shall return once more,
> To know that deep love of the Goddess.
> The spirit is gone; therefore,
> Let the man who stood for that spirit be freed also!

The Priestess covers her head once more with her shawl and she takes up a sharp knife and the pot of corn. The Priestess cuts the corn with her knife - this symbolically represents the cutting of the last wheatsheaf in the fields. The Priestess turns to face the coven and says:

As day follows night, this must come to pass.
For all things must rise and fall;
Only the Goddess remains the same.
Thus the rite is done, the price paid, the sacrifice taken;
But from the ashes, a new life shall spring forth.
Takest thou each a seed and grow it
And bring back a seed
From the corn that grows from it!

Each member of the coven takes a grain of wheat and the Priestess calls:

Now is not the time for sorrow,
He has died to give us life.
Let us once more tread the dance,
But in joy and understanding.
Let us leave here happy within - Rejoice!

This time the dance is to be lively. After the dance, the ceremony of the cakes and wine is enacted, after which the Priestess calls for the feast. At the end of the evening the circle is closed in the usual manner.

MABON
(AUTUMN EQUINOX)

The festival of Mabon is held between Sept. 21st and 23rd. Mabon marks the middle of autumn and is the third festival of light and also the autumn equinox. At this time of year, Llew the God of Light is defeated by his darker brother Goronwy. Llew, who is born at the winter solstice as the child of promise, increases in his strength with the lengthening days. However, after the summer solstice, when the days shorten, he slowly becomes weaker until after the third day of the autumn equinox when his darker brother is able to defeat him.

THE RITE

Any autumn flowering plants can be used to adorn the room and the cauldron. For this rite, a solar crown and a weapon are required.

The circle is cast in the correct manner and the God and the Goddess are invoked into the Priest and Priestess. The Priestess begins the rite with the legend of the time when the God of Sunlight lost the battle with the God of Darkness:

> **Witches all, we are gathered here this night**
> **In the midst of autumn.**
> **Now is the time of balance**
> **When night and day face each other as equals.**
> **Shortly the day shall wane and the night shall begin to wax.**
> **The balance shifts in favour of the Dark God**
> **And the God of Sunlight weakens with each passing minute.**

It is now possible for his dark twin to defeat him.
And so it has come to pass that the Sun God
Is brought low by the God of Darkness,
Who now sits upon the throne of his brother,
And begins his dark reign for the winter.

The Priestess calls aloud:

Where is he who impersonates the Sun God?

The man chosen for the role of the Sun God steps forward and the Priestess addresses him:

Thou art the Sun God;
Lord of the Waning year.
Maiden, bring his crown!

The Sun God is then crowned, given his weapon and placed in the centre of the circle facing west. The Priestess calls:

Where is he that impersonates the Dark Lord?

The man who impersonates the Dark God steps forward and the Priestess addresses him:

Thou art the Dark Lord,
God of the Waxing year!

The Dark Lord then stands in the centre of the circle facing the Sun God. The Priestess calls:

With the Sun God growing weaker,
The waxing of the year is accomplished.
And the reign of the Sun God is ended.
With the Dark Lord growing more powerful,
Comes the waning of the year.
The Dark Lord must now defeat his brother
Who is the Lord of Sunlight,
To take his rightful place on the throne
Until his brother the Sun God
Shall return once more as the child of promise!

The Dark Lord says unto his brother the Sun God:

Thou hast had thy time of dominion,
Will thou stand before the Dark Lord whom I represent?

The Sun God replies:

I cannot, for it is ordained,
As darkness yields to light,
So light must yield to darkness.
Therefore, do I yield to thee my power.

The Sun God kneels before the Dark Lord and yields his sword to him, and the Dark Lord takes it from him. The Sun God then rises and crowns the Dark Lord with his solar crown. The Sun God says to his brother:

To thee with love do I yield my reign.

The Dark Lord replies:

I do thank thee, but I ask of thee
One more gift before you depart, light the fire
So that joy of life and magic be ours once more
For one night.

The Sun God lights the candle in the cauldron and retires to sit in the west of the circle where he is covered with a shawl.

The Priestess calls aloud:

Farewell O Sun, ever-returning light.
The Lord of Light now departs to the land of youth
Through the gates of death,
To dwell enthroned, the judge of men and Gods,
The horned leader of the creatures of the earth.
Yet as he stands unseen without the circle,
So dwelleth he within the secret seed;
The seed of new reaped grain,
The seed of flesh

Hidden in earth, the wonderful seed of the stars.
In him is life, and life is the light of man.
That which was never born, never dies.
Therefore the wise ones weep not, but rejoice.

The Sun God rejoins the circle for the ceremony of the cakes and wine. Afterwards, the Priestess calls for the feast. At the end of the evening the circle is dissolved.

SAMHAIN
(HALLOWEEN)

The festival of Samhain is the last Fire Festival of the pagan year. Samhain is also known as All Hallows Eve and is celebrated on October 31st. Samhain is the night of all-souls and is a time of great mourning. All Hallows Eve is believed by pagans to be a night that is outside time. At this time of the year the doors to the underworld are thrown open and spirits are thought to roam the earth. It is the custom at this time of year to place food offerings outside the house to encourage dead relatives to come and join the living for the celebrations. Due to the emotional nature of this rite there are no new members admitted. Halloween is celebrated in remembrance of the God of the Corn who sacrificed himself at Lughnasad for the sake of others. Samhain is therefore, a remembrance service for the God of Vegetation who has departed from the earth. This is the time when all those who have died are remembered.

THE RITE

The altar is adorned with branches of yew, the tree of immortality, some apples, nuts and ivy. By the altar are apples, cider, and a candle for each person attending the rite. A candle is placed in the cauldron.

Some covens at this time of the year appoint a Lord of Misrule. The Lord of Misrule is given a balloon on a stick, which is the symbol of the Jester. He is then proclaimed as the Lord of Misrule. The Lord of Misrule represents the season of Chaos and it is his job to bring chaos into the circle. The title of Lord of Chaos is mostly given for the winter. At the end of the winter season, he steps down.

The circle is cast in the traditional manner and the coven go to stand in a circle around the cauldron. After a short while, the Priestess, who is dressed in black, lights the candle in the cauldron and calls:

I call thee, O thou that impersonates the Dark God.

The Priest steps forward and he responds with:

I hear and I come my Lady.

The Priest is crowned with the horned helmet and is given a sword. The Priestess addresses him:

Lord of Shadows,
God of Life and giver of life;
Knowledge of thee,
Is knowledge of death!
Open wide I pray thee,
The gates through which all must pass.
Let our dear ones who have gone before us
Return this night to make merry with us.
And when our time comes, as it must,
O thou the comforter, the consoler,
The giver of peace and rest,
We will enter thy realms gladly and unafraid.
For we know that once rested and refreshed
Amongst our loved ones, we too shall be reborn
Through thy grace,
And the grace of the Great Mother.
Let it be in the same time and place as our dear ones
And may we meet, know, and remember
And love them once again.
On this night, the holy eve of Samhain,
Descend we pray thee, into this,
The body of thy servant and High Priest!

The Priestess gives him the fivefold salute and he responds with:

I do thank thee my Lady,
And in my duties shall I ever
Give thanks to thee!

The Priest addresses the coven:

O thou of the ancient craft,
The day has passed and the Oak King is dead.
The earth awaits the return of life.
As darkness follows light,
So winter shall follow summer.
Snow must fall and winter's darkness come.
For seven moons shall the Dark Lord have dominion,
Until the return once more of life to the land.
On this night in ages past was the year's ending.
At this time of the year,
The doors to the underworld were thrown open,
And the spirits were everywhere just as they are now.
The almighty dead return from their graves
Remembering warmth, comfort and joy of friends.
So witches all, give honour and love
To those that have passed into the Summerland.
Let us dance and make merry
For those that have gone before us,
We invite them to come forth
And to join us in the circle as they once did in life.
The old has passed away,
And the new is yet to come.
Now is the time to shed sorrow
And renew hope for the year to come.
As I do dance so shalt thou follow!

The Priest then leads the coven in a dance, leading them out of the room. On their way out, each member of the coven is given a candle by the Priestess. After the coven have left the room, the Priest returns and lights his candle from the one in the cauldron. He then opens the door and beckons to the coven to enter. He asks each person in turn as they enter the room:

What dost thou want of me?

They reply: **Light to help us see beyond.**

The Priest answers: **As ye pass so shall light be given.**

As they pass him in single file, the Priest lights their tapers. The coven awaits him in the centre of the room where they stand gathered around the cauldron. Once they are all in the room, the Priest leads the procession anticlockwise, slowly spiralling into the centre of the circle. At the entrance to the underworld (centre of the circle) the Priestess in her shawl appears (as the Dark Goddess). The coven gather around the cauldron and sit down on the floor. The Dark Goddess addresses the coven:

Let us think of those that we loved
Who have passed on to the Summerland.
Let each of us place a token of remembrance
In the cauldron before us,
For one day we shall want others to do likewise for us.

All the candles are put into the cauldron and the members of the coven sit and meditate upon the lights in the cauldron. The coven recall memories of those who have passed on to the summerland. After a while, a bell is rung to signal the end of the meditation. The crone calls to the Priest:

Go once more, and lead my
People back across the river.

The Priest then leads the procession out of the room and back in again as he did before, but this time the procession travels clockwise. The Priestess leaves the room and discards the guise of the crone. On her return to the room the Priestess closes the gateway and the ceremony of wine and cakes is performed. After the ceremony of the cakes and wine, food is placed on the doorstep for a gift to the dear departed.

The Priestess then calls: **Let the feast begin.**

The festivities then ensue. Apple bobbing and trick or treating is customary at this time of the year. After the feast is over, the circle is closed in the traditional manner.

YULE
(WINTER SOLSTICE)

Yule is the last Festival of Light and is celebrated after dawn between December 21st and 23rd. At this time of the year, it is the middle of winter and the Dark Lord rules supreme. However, the Sun God is now reborn as the Child of Promise (promise of the return of warmth). Yule is the festival of the holy infant and is called Christmas by Christians. The nativity play that is enacted at this time of the year originates from the East. In Babylon, the child of promise is called Tammuz and in Egypt, the child is called Harpocrates (Harpe-krat).

It is the custom at this time of the year to exchange gifts (this arises from the tradition of bringing gifts to the Holy Child). Pinchi witch is one of the traditional games played at this time of the year (this is where someone blackens their fingers secretly, then pinches the cheek of the person sitting next to them).

THE RITE

For this rite, mistletoe, a Yule log, some tapers, a solar crown, and a child (or doll) are required. A cauldron containing a candle is placed in the centre of the room and the circle is cast in the traditional manner. The rite begins in partial darkness with only the central candle burning, and after a short pause for silence, the Priestess calls aloud:

Where is he that impersonates the Holly King?

The man who impersonates the Holly King steps forward and the Priestess addresses him:

Thou art the Holly King, God of the Waning year,
Maiden, bring his crown!

The Priestess crowns him. The Holly King then stands in the centre of the circle. The Priestess calls:

Where is he that impersonates the Oak King?

The person who has been chosen to represent the Oak King then steps forward. The Priestess addresses him:

Thou art the Oak King, God of the Waxing year,
Maiden, bring his crown!

The Priestess crowns him. The Priestess then places them both in the centre of the circle and asks them to face one another. While this is done, the Priest has laid down on the floor in the west of the circle. The Holly King asks:

My brother and I have been arrayed for battle,
But where is our Lord, the Sun?

The Priest returns solemnly:

Our Lord the Sun is dead!

The Priestess places the shawl over her head and calls:

Return O return, O God of the Sun.
God of the light return!
Thine enemies have fled, there are no more enemies.
O lovely helper return, return,
Return to thy sister, thy wife, who loveth thee!
O my brother, my consort, my love,
Return; return, when I see thee not,
My heart grieves for thee!
Mine eyes seek for thee!
My feet roam the earth in search of thee!
Gods and men both weep for thee!
God of the Sun return,

Return once more to thy wife,
Thy sister, who loveth thee!

The Priestess then makes several circuits of the temple searching for her lost love and discovers his body. The Priestess kneels and embraces the body of the God. The coven call:

Queen of heaven, Queen of earth,
Bring to us the Child of Promise.

The coven uncovers the Priest and the Priestess pulls him to his feet. The Priestess calls:

Golden sunshine in the morn,
The Sun God is reborn.
Spring come fast, all sorrow past,
Blessed be the Goddess!

The Priestess calls:

Now in the depths of winter,
The waning of the year is accomplished.
And the reign of the Holly King is over.
The Sun God is reborn and
The waxing of the year begins.
The Oak King must slay his brother the Holly King
And rule over the land until the height of summer,
When his brother shall rise again.

The two Gods grip each other by the shoulders and a struggle takes place. Eventually the Oak King forces the Holly King onto his knees. The Priestess then blindfolds the Holly King and dances around him. While the Priestess dances, the Priest sings the song:

Dance Lady dance, on the Holly King's tomb,
Dance Lady dance, at the Oak King's birth,
Dance Lady dance, to the Sun God's power,
Dance Lady dance, for the Holly King's passing.
Dance Lady dance, for the Oak King's triumph,
Dance Lady dance, for the Sun God's glory,
Dance Lady dance, to the sun on high,
Dance Lady dance, to the year's long tide!

The Holly King is then led blindfold to a corner of the room. The Priestess addresses the coven:

The spirit of the Holly King has gone from us,
To rest in the castle of the silver wheel.
Until with the turning of the year, the season shall come
When he shall return again to rule.
The spirit is gone, therefore
Let the man that stood for that spirit be freed also.

The High Priestess calls:

Let the Midwinter fires shine forth!

The Oak King lights the candle in the cauldron. The Priestess leaves the room and after a short pause, a whisper spreads around the coven from person to person:

A child is born!

The Priestess returns to the room carrying a small child (this can be a baby or a doll) and she proclaims aloud:

Lo, it is the Child of Promise!
It is the Great Mother who has given him birth!
He is the Lord our Sun who is born again.
Set aside all darkness and tears,
And look instead to the coming year!

The Priestess then calls:

Come ye of the joyous craft and join me in the dance!

The coven dance and the Priestess calls for the feast. The members of the coven then give gifts to the Child of Promise and merriment ensues. After the feast is over, the circle is closed. It is the tradition at this time of the year to exchange small Yule presents.

CHAPTER SEVEN

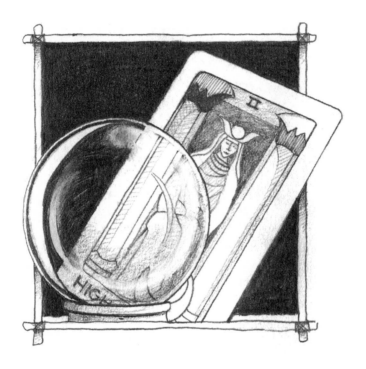

THE EIGHTFOLD WAY

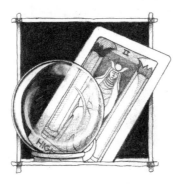

With the forming of the religious pantheons, the Gods became identified as groups. These groups of Gods then became associated with numbers and the numbers in turn developed a religious meaning. Depending upon the religion of the period, these numbers were regarded as either lucky or unlucky. The belief then arose that certain days of the year also became lucky or unlucky according to their numbers. This belief was later expanded upon by Pythagoras who created geometrical figures from the sacred numbers.

In keeping with the ancient tradition, Wiccans also regard numbers to have magical powers. It is not the number that is important, but the power that the number represents. In Wicca, the numbers three, five and eight are most important. Most things in Wicca revolve around these numbers.

1. The number one is a number of masculine energy, and it represents the reproductive powers of the phallus. The number one is also the number of the Horned God.

2. The number two represents passive feminine energy and the regenerative powers of the womb. The number two is the number of the Green Goddess and also represents harmonious balance. Two is also a number that represents dualities and the uniting of two individuals.

3. The number three represents the three phases of the moon and the holy trinities, especially that of the man, woman and the child. Three is the number of the White Goddess and the foundations of the earth (sky, sea and earth). The geometric representation of the number three is the triangle.

4. The cosmic cube (square) represents the number four. Four is the number of the four supports of heaven (4 elemental beings or angels) and represents mercy and wisdom.

5. The pentagram represents the number five. The number five, represents fire and aggression, it also the number of birthdays of the Gods. Five also represents the senses of sight, smell, hearing, taste and touch.

6. The Hexagram represents the number six. The number Six represents the Sun and its regenerative powers, (health and wealth).

7. The heptagram represents the number seven, which represents the stars of the Great Bear. Seven is also the number of the Great Mother and the Goddess of Love.

8. The octagram represents the number eight. The number eight is associated with spiders, the messengers of the Gods, and chaos. The sun wheel, which is the symbol of the Babylonian Sun God Samas, is depicted with eight arms, as is the Wiccan wheel, which is the symbol of the Wiccan Year. However, the ancient Greeks regarded the eight-armed symbol as a symbol of chaos. The Greeks, therefore, associate the number eight with chaos magic (otherwise known as octarine magic). The number eight also represents the Ogdoad - who were the ancient Gods of Khemmis.

9. The enneagram represents the number nine. The number nine represents the Ennead — the nine ancient Gods of Egypt and the moon (as a multiple of 3 x 3).

10. The decagram represents the number ten. The number ten in Jewish mysticism represents the spheres of the Sephirotic Tree - see any book on Kabbalah

THE EIGHTFOLD WAY

In the craft of Wicca, there are eight ways of raising power within the circle; this is called the Eightfold way. The eightfold way is described as the eight-spoked wheel upon which Wicca turns. The eight ways of raising power are:

1. MENTAL ABILITY.

Power can be raised through meditation, trance, and the application of pure will (mind over matter).

2. SPEECH.

Power can be raised within the circle through the rituals, the chants, and the spells. It is the belief that sound can penetrate the veil into the other world, but for this to work properly, chants must be hypnotic and invocations powerful. All intentions must be voiced clearly so that the Gods may understand the purpose of the rite.

3. HALLUCINOGENS.

The use of wine, incense, essential oils and 'soft' drugs have all been used in the past as ways of helping the mind to focus. This is an ancient shamanic method of achieving magical results. The shamans used hallucinogenics to aid visualization and to help them shape-shift. Among the many substances that were once used were: thorn apple, henbane, belladonna, fly agaric, psilocybin, mescal buttons, pokeroot, hemp, wormwood, aconitum and opium poppy.

4. DANCE.

Dance is perhaps the most widely used of all the methods of raising power. In this way physical energy can be expended for magical result. The dances in Wicca vary according to the rite. There are the spiral dance, the wheel dance, the maze dance and the dance of the Lame God.

5. VOTIVE OFFERINGS

Offerings are often made in ritual supplications to the Gods to obtain good favour. An offering is not acceptable unless the supplicant is actually surrendering something they will need - this is the nature of sacrifice. A blood offering was also not valid unless the blood was their own blood or that of an animal that they owned.

To obtain answers to vital questions, some Wiccans summon spirits. This is called Goetic invocation. Spirits cannot usually be seen, because they require blood to obtain substance. In very hazy conditions the spirits can sometimes just be seen in the incense smoke. Never expect a spirit to appear directly in front of you. You must use your senses to detect the spirit and order it into the triangle of art (see the Goetia by DeLawrence) before a conversation can take place. The spirit must be banished before the circle is closed; failure to do so can be catastrophic. In Wicca, bloodless offerings of bread, wine and incense are made to obtain the blessings of the God and Goddess.

6. THE SCOURGE

The scourge can be used to beat power into an object — such as the pentacle, or to purify through pain. Witches of old were known to slap their bodies to heighten their awareness. In the Middle East, flagellation was also used as a form of ritual purification. The ancient Shamans were also known to use pain as a focus and would crucify themselves on trees to induce prophetic visions.

7. THE GREAT RITE

In Wicca, sex is a sacrament and the conjoining of a man with a woman is regarded as a merging of two great powers. A vast amount of sexual energy is raised during the sexual act; this is used by some covens as an alternative way of raising power. The lunar tides run stronger in women than they do in men but through conjunction during the full moon, some of this power can be absorbed (in Wicca, sexual acts are private and are never witnessed).

8. THOUGHT-FORMS

Visualisation in magic is very important. Through visualisation the witch can become acquainted with the God-forms. For the practice of visualisation, the five senses all need to be employed. For example; if you wish to visualise a rose, you must see the image of the rose in every detail, then you must visualise yourself holding the rose. Feel the stem beneath your fingers. Visualise yourself smelling the rose, smell its perfume. Next try to hear the sounds of a rose garden, then taste the rose and image yourself in the rose garden. If your imagination is good you can mentally project yourself into another place in this way. This technique can be used to visualise the Gods and Goddesses standing before you. It can also be used to mentally teleport yourself to a safe place while sitting in a protective circle.

THE FIVE INTENTIONS

In conjunction with the eightfold way there are five magical intentions. They are:

1. Magical intent: The purpose of the rite must be clearly defined before the circle begins and the plan must be followed to the letter.

2. Ritual preparation: All must be properly prepared beforehand.

3. The Invocation: Spirits must be invoked with authority and respect.

4. Consecration: All tools must be properly prepared and anointed. Patchouli, sandalwood and Abra-melin are the oils mostly used in Wicca.

5. Purification: Participants in the rite must be properly bathed before the rite.

THE WICCAN REDE

The Wiccan rede is another of the eightfold ways of Wicca. The Wiccan rede is the code of ethics by which all Wiccans abide. The laws of Wicca are very simple:

Eight words the Wiccan rede fulfills
Do as thou wilt - but harm thou none!

1. Seek not to use your magic to harm others, nor destroy that which you cannot obtain, for this will only bring sadness upon you.

2. Seek not to take revenge - 'to slap knee, hip, and thigh' or be forced into hasty action. All things are cyclic and those who sow shall eventually reap their just reward on the wheel of karma.

3. Do not take the things that belong to the God and Goddess and harm not the creatures of the earth.

4. Concern yourself not with selfish things, but with healing and helping others.

5. Seek to encourage gentle change to happen and do not be tempted to force change, for this is the way of chaos.
6. Sacrifice no living thing, nor offer up that which is not yours.

7. Seek not to use your magic for the amusement of others, lest you become the plaything of the Gods.

8. Seek not to control the freedom of others, lest you be controlled yourself.

ASTROLOGY

The Ancients believed that their lives were written in the stars and believed that by studying them, they could come to understand their past, present and future. Most Wiccans are trained in Astrology and are able to predict the most favourable times for casting spells to obtain the best results. A knowledge of astronomy is also important because the nature of each planet in our solar system is represented in a God-form.

DIVINATION

The need to predict the future arose from the need to know the intentions of the Gods. It was the belief that only through knowing the intentions of the Gods could supplication be made and catastrophe avoided. Wiccans use several methods of divining the future and they are all trained in some form of divination. Divination can be made through the use of reflective surfaces as mirrors. These help the diviner to see pictures or symbols in their mind. For the purpose of divination, crystals, magic mirrors, water in the cauldron, Tarot cards, candles and runestones can be used. The diviner does not really see beyond, but inwards, because it is there; that the powers of extra sensory perception dwell.

OBTAINING SECOND SIGHT

ESP can be obtained through astral travel or scrying. In the art of scrying, the diviner sits in a comfortable position seated before the object they are using. The diviner relaxes while gazing fixedly on the object i.e., a candle flame; the diviner then enters a partial trance whereby the only thing they can see is the tool of divination. Over a period of time, the diviner will begin to see images form in their mind that appear to be in the divinatory tool. The images that the scryer sees may not necessarily be comprehensible at the time, but should perhaps be analyzed at a later time. When the diviner becomes tired they must stop scrying and bring their gaze away from the divinatory tool.

ASTRAL TRAVELLING

Knowledge of the past, present and future can often be obtained through astral travel. In Wicca there is a method of training the astral body to leave the physical body at will. Astral travelling to obtain second sight (knowledge of the future) is common practice among witches. Those who wish to learn the techniques of astral travel are asked to lay comfortably face down on chairs, with their stomach, thighs and chest supported. The arms are then extended in front and secured. The trainee is whipped with the scourge which is dragged backwards toward their head. If the trainee tries to make their astral body fall forwards with the movement of the scourge, it will be easy for the astral body to be dragged forwards out of the physical body.

Another way to astral travel is to sit in front of a mirror and look at your image. Close your eyes and imagine your mirror image as a glowing body of light (thought-form). Now transfer your mind (consciousness) into the image in the mirror. From the image in the mirror, look out across at your physical body. Eventually when you can accomplish this, seek to control the movements and the travels of the image. To return to your body just think of your feet. During your travels it is important to remember all that you see.

Chapter Eight

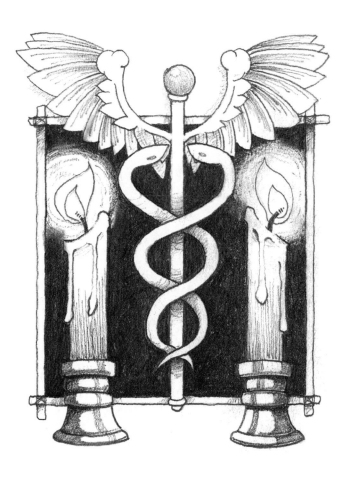

The Planetary Rites

The planetary rites of Wicca were written as ritual plays in the tradition of the ancients. Aleister Crowley also wrote and performed modern variations of these rites, which he called the Rites of Eleusis. The Rites of Eleusis were performed in much the same way as the ancients performed their rituals, with people acting out the roles of the Gods.

To understand the planetary rites, it is necessary to have an understanding of the natures of the planets and the God-forms that accompany them. Familiarity with the God-forms can be gained by reading the myths and legends of the Greek and Roman Gods. The God-forms are only representations of the natures of the planets in human form - this makes them easier to identify with.

The planetary rituals must be performed upon the day and if possible, upon the hour assigned to the God that is to be invoked. Any colours and metals given in the rituals must be strictly adhered to if possible.

There is a table of planetary workings that is used by Wiccans to calculate the day and the times for their planetary workings. This table is given in the Key of Solomon. The first hour after midnight always belongs to the ruling planet of the day.

THE RITE OF MERCURY

The Rite of Mercury can be performed anytime during the full or the waxing phase of the moon, and upon the times allocated to Mercury (see tables of hours). Wednesday is the day allocated to the messengers of the Gods, therefore the Wiccan rituals for communication, eloquence and wit are held on Wednesday evenings.

PREPARATION FOR THE RITE

The incense that is to be burned must be sharp and light. The altar cloth, the candles and the ceremonial attire should all correspond to the rite (these must be pale yellow, multicolours or black and white). Dual colours are associated with the messenger Gods because they are androgynous and are children of both light and darkness. As hermaphrodites, the messenger Gods represent the unification of male and female. The God Mercury is usually invoked to obtain the skills of eloquence, wit, diplomacy, healing, writing and science. All the messenger Gods have the power to travel between the worlds because they are children born from both light and darkness.

Alloyed metals are sacred to the messenger Gods i.e., aluminium and brass, (because they are combinations) and should be used if possible. For this rite, you will need a Caduceus (the healing wand of mercury), a horn and a quill pen. The mood for the rite should be alert and electric.

THE CIRCLE CONJURATION

The circle is cast in the usual manner and the Priest blows the horn eight times to signal the beginning of the rite.

156

The Priestess begins the dance by taking hold of the hand of the Priest. The Priest in turn takes the hand of the woman nearest him. This continues until all the coven has joined the dance. As the coven dance, the chant is called:

> **The horn, the horn, we hear the horn,**
> **Sounding shrill and sweet.**
> **The call, the call, we hear the call,**
> **Compelling us to meet.**
> **Quick, quick, we must be quick,**
> **To glimpse his silver form;**
> **Darting here, darting there,**
> **His errands to perform!**
> **Glad, glad, our hearts are glad,**
> **To know he's on his way!**
> **A beauteous form with eyes of blue,**
> **And golden curls astray.**

At the call of **"Down!"** The coven all drop to the floor. After a pause for breath the Priest calls:

> **Write a love song, play the pipes,**
> **Revel in thy mirth.**
> **He will hear and soon attend**
> **Our circle here on earth!**

The Priest takes up the Caduceus and calls:

> **Whosoever wishes aid**
> **Within the powers of Mercury,**
> **Listen to my words - be alert,**
> **Be wise, be learned, be not biased,**
> **And scoff not at the truth;**
> **For thou art the fool!**

The Priest lays down the wand and hands each person a piece of paper and a pencil with the words:

> **Upon this paper shall you write,**
> **What you require upon this night!**

The coven write down any wishes that they would like to come true. Mercurial charms can be made, job applications can be filled in, or letters of correspondence can be written. The papers are then gathered in, the petitions are separated from the correspondence and the charms (because these will be burned to pass the wish). Holding the petitions aloft, the Priest addresses the coven:

> **The petitions I hold are the wishes of us all,**
> **Like newborn babes.**
> **Do we dare to give them life?**

The coven answer:

> **Aye!**

The Priest answers:

> **So be it!**
> **We shall release them**
> **Into the care of Mercury!**

The Priest then burns the petitions in the cauldron - which has been brought into the circle by the Priestess. The Priest takes up the Caduceus and holds it aloft as the petitions burn and the Priestess marks any letters that have been written with the symbol of Mercury. The Priestess recites the spell for the aid of Mercury:

> **Fire light, fire bright,**
> **Twisted snakes of black and white,**
> **Uphold thy rod unto our sight,**
> **Lend to us thy healing light.**
> **Bring us wisdom, bring us speed,**
> **Help us in our time of need.**

After the rite, the circle is closed in the usual fashion and the candle is left to burn down. The letters are posted before dawn.

THE RITE OF MARS

Mars is the Roman God of War and he is portrayed as a giant, red-hued, armour-clad warrior and the embodiment of masculinity. Not all of us are born bold, courageous, aggressive, strong willed, or physically strong, but by calling upon Mars, the ancient God of War, some of these warrior qualities can be obtained for protection in battle. The Rites of Mars can be enacted at times when danger threatens and battles loom. The powers of Mars are often depicted as the ram, renowned for his determination, aggression and sexual drive. No women are present for this rite.

PREPARATION FOR THE RITE

The rites of Mars can be performed upon the full, or the waxing phase of the moon, but should correctly be enacted upon the day or the hours allotted to the Gods of War (see tables of hours and the table of correspondences).

The altar cloth, the candles, and the robes should be red if possible. The incense burned must have a hot smell (tobacco, pepper etc.). Iron and steel are the metals that are to be used for this rite. The Sword of Power must be beneath the altar along with a six-foot pole (battle staff). Pine branches and pinecones may be placed upon the altar along with the phallic wand. A gong or a bell is also required for this rite.

THE CIRCLE CONJURATION

The coven are to assemble in silence. The mood of the rite is serious and resilient. The coven sits cross-legged on the floor in a circle,

159

silent, and upright. The coven cross their arms over their chests and make fists with their hands. The participants are to breathe deeply, building up their energy levels. Before the rite begins, the Priest will address the coven and explain the nature of the rite:

> **The rites of Mars are enacted**
> **To acquire strength and fortitude**
> **During times of strife.**
> **The powers bestowed by Mars**
> **Are those of fortitude, strength, desire,**
> **And victory in the forthcoming battle!**

The Priest then casts the circle in the usual manner and goes to stand in the centre of the circle. The Priest signals the beginning of the rite with the striking of a gong.

At the sound of the gong, (or bell) the coven stand and join hands above their heads (in the centre of the circle). The dance then follows with the coven walking sideways with a stamp of the left foot (this can be performed to the beat of a drum). The Priest dons the horned helmet and calls aloud:

> **Are thou all of true heart?**

They reply:

> **Aye!**

The Priest calls:

> **Be thou all of true will?**

They reply:

> **Aye!**

The Priest calls:

> **Be thou all of sound wind and limb?**

They reply:

> **Aye!**

The Priest calls:

> **Then fear naught under the heaven but the Gods!**

The Priest then strikes the gong to end the dance and the dancers stand still. The Priest then takes up the staff in his right hand and goes to the centre of the circle. At the centre of the circle the Priest raises up the staff and calls:

> **By the powers of the God Mars**
> **May we be endowed.**
> **Lift up the staff of life,**
> **The staff that governs us all!**

The Priest calls:

> **Grasp ye the symbol of life and strength,**
> **And give it recognition.**
> **Circle now in the wheel of life,**
> **With fortitude and with courage!**

Each person takes hold of the staff with their right hand. Still facing the centre of the circle and the staff, the Priest places his left hand upon the right shoulder of the person to the left of him. All the coven do likewise and at a nod of the Priest's head, they march sideways in the direction of the sun. As the members of the coven step sideways in unison, they stamp with their left foot. The Priest chanting a spell for strength:

> **Around this symbol we do tread,**
> **Fearing naught that lies ahead.**
> **Courage within us brightly burns,**
> **As this wheel of witches turns,**
> **Step by step, round we go,**
> **Straight of back, top to toe,**
> **As we tread the measure proud,**
> **One and all we shout aloud.**
> **Make us as this rod so high,**
> **Balanced between earth and sky.**

After the chant has been recited three times, the coven releases the staff. The Priest takes the staff in both hands and proclaims aloud:

> **There is work to be done tonight;**
> **Let us set to the task.**

Talismans of power for protection in battle can then be made from parchment (paper) and red ink - or any material that is sacred to the

Gods of War. Spells for protection are then burned in the cauldron, and any talismans that have been made are consecrated.

After the magical working the Priest takes up the staff and calls aloud:

> **Cleanse our souls upon this night,**
> **And fill us all with hopeful light.**
> **Treadest thou with lightened step,**
> **May all our fears be truly met.**
> **Swiftly calmed and strongly healed,**
> **As the warrior in the field!**

The staff is then laid down and the circle is closed in the usual manner.

THE RITE OF THE MOON

The Rite of the Moon is performed to obtain the gifts of enchantment and prophecy. For this rite, the circle may be cast during the full or the waxing phase of the moon, or upon the day and the hour allotted to the Goddess of the Moon (Monday)

For this rite, the incense burned must be of a cool, clean, lunar nature. The altar cloth, candles and robes, must all be either silver or white (the colours of the moon). The temple should be strewn with willow branches or any flowers sacred to the moon. For this rite you will need a systrum or a tambourine. Silver is the metal assigned to the moon, and is believed to have the power (as does crystal and glass) to harness the power of the moon. Items of silver and crystal may be worn during this ritual to receive a magical charge. As silver goods are expensive, glass may be used to good effect and replace any metal objects that would normally be used.

The Goddess of the Moon is believed to hold the keys that unlock the mysteries and to possess the secrets of enchantment.

As Diana, she is said to possess the powers of divination, prophecy, enchantment and dreaming. She is also said to rule all the tides that be. Diana is worshipped as a Goddess of renewal and rebirth (she renews herself each month) and as a great mother. For the rites of Diana, the circle is cast in the usual manner.

THE RITE

The Priestess signals the beginning of the rite by shaking her systrum. A young woman who represents the White Goddess as a maiden enters the circle and stands in the centre (she must wear a white robe with a flower tiara) where she proclaims:

Chaste am I when first you see
The silver bow behind the tree,
In this guise men come to me,
I am the essence of mystery.

A mature woman (or woman pretending to be pregnant) enters the circle (she wears a green robe and a garland of flowers) she represents the Goddess in her prime. The woman who represents the mother goes to stand in the centre of the circle and the virgin bride disappears. The mother declares:

Fertile giver of life am I,
Yet all who live are bound to die.
Perfection in me, shown to be,
The mother of all, on land or sea!

The pregnant woman disappears and is replaced by an aged lady who represents the crone (she wears a black robe with a shawl over her head concealing her face). The crone proclaims:

I am the dark one - now behold,
All the secrets I enfold.
If my image thou canst bear
And the abyss thou wilt dare.
The silver path shall then be thine,
To lead thee to my secret shrine!

The two other Goddesses then enter the circle and all three embrace. Together they rotate in a circle clockwise nine times (in imitation of the passage of the moon). They all chant:

Three in one and one in three,
The oldest form of Trinity!

The three Goddesses then lead the spiral dance to the chant:

Dark to light and light to dark
Across the sky a-turning,
We of the craft do understand,

Our faith in thee affirming!
Show to us thy silver light,
Life and all it's meaning.
Guide us in your secret ways,
Mistress of all dreaming!
Ruler of the hearth and home,
Lady of the tides,
All our days are blessed by thee,
While the earth abides!
When the silver cord is cut,
In the astral light,
The river we shall cross to thee,
Once more in thy sight!

The Priestess goes to the altar and kneels before the cauldron filled with water. She dedicates it to the Goddess with the words:

Lady of the Moon, I am thy daughter,
Bless this, thine own element of water,
Precious fluid of life it be,
Given to us by Goddess' three.

The Priestess then fills a cup from the cauldron.

The maiden calls: **Let it be filled with purity and light.**

The mother calls: **Let it be filled with fertility and abundance!**

The crone calls: **I give all who partake of it, wisdom and inspiration.**

Each of the Goddesses drinks in turn from the cup, beginning with the maiden and ending with the crone. They pass each other the cup with the kiss and the blessing. The cup is then passed to the coven so they may drink also. The three Goddesses lead a dance to the witch's rune. At a signal from the Priestess, the dance ceases and the cauldron of water is brought into the centre of the circle.

The Priestess calls:

Come to the image of the moon
And look into her face.
Revelations she may show
By her special grace,

165

> Memories of another mask
> Thy soul has worn before.
> Symbols, signs, and omens show
> What fate has yet in store!

The coven seat themselves around the cauldron and look inside it. The Priestess calls:

> O moon of moods we follow thee.
> In the dark, thy light a-shining;
> Fill us all with visions rare,
> Mistress of all dreaming!

> Draw us with thine argent light
> Through the crescent gate,
> So we may come by night to thee,
> O Lady of our fate.

The Priestess addresses the coven:

> Look into the darkened surface.
> Past or present may be glimpsed
> And things still yet to come!

After a short meditation upon the surface of the water, the Priestess signals the end of the meditation with a clap of her hands. During the period that follows, tarot cards may be read and scrying may be practiced using a variety of objects. At the end of the evening the circle is closed in the usual manner.

THE RITE OF SATURN

The planet Saturn is dark, heavy and cold, and is the slowest of all the planets. Saturn is not only regarded as a God of the cold and dark earth, but also as a God of destiny and time, and because the cold earth is incapable of sustaining life, Saturn also becomes a God of death and destruction. All the Gods who represent death, are assigned to the underworld where they watch over the souls of the dead until it is time for them to be reborn. In Wicca, the God who rules the underworld is known as *The Lord of the Hills and Mounds* because in ancient times the dead were buried in mounds. The Gods of the Underworld are only able to leave their domain once the Gods of Life have withdrawn. The Gods of Chaos are then set free for the seasons of destruction, i.e., wintertime. Although the Dark Gods of the underworld are generally regarded as evil, they are not, for they are part of the cycle of life and they clear the way for new growth. The Dark Gods are also regarded as Gods of Fire and firelight, because it is the belief that they supply light to the souls of the dead while they sojourn in the underworld. All the Saturnine Gods are keepers of cosmic law and order, and they have dominion over time and destiny. The dark rites (cursing rituals) of the God Saturn are not performed in Wicca and the Gods of Darkness are only called upon to gain knowledge of time and destiny (they are also called upon to open the doors to the underworld on All Hallows Eve).

PREPARATION FOR THE RITE

The ritual for Saturn may be performed during the dark or waning phase of the moon, or during the times allocated to the Saturnine Gods (see table of hours and the table of correspondences). The altar must face to the west (toward the Underworld) for this rite. The altar cloth, candles, and robes should be black in colour and the incense burned should be of a dark, heavy, musky type (candles in the room should be sufficient in number as to give adequate light for the ritual). Some small candles, paper, black ink and a small offering are required for this rite. Lead is the metal of Saturn and any talismans that are to be made must be constructed from lead or black ink on paper.

THE RITE

The coven enters the temple in sombre mood and sit silently in a circle. The Priestess, who wears a shawl over her head and holds a black candle, stands in the centre of the circle. The Priestess then breaks the silence with a warning:

> **Ye who look upon the flame remember well its origins.**
> **Out of the womb of time it is born an innocent babe.**
> **Consider well thy purpose here tonight,**
> **Keep thy thoughts pure, and free from malice.**

A male member of the coven goes to light the watchtowers and the rest of the candles with a taper. The Priestess then puts the candle down upon the altar and casts the circle in the usual manner. After the circle conjuration, the Priestess addresses the coven:

> **I am she, who was;**
> **Before all life was created.**
> **I am the one who brought light into darkness.**
> **I am the Great Mother.**
> **Consider well thy purpose!**

The Priestess then whispers the intention of the rite, which had already been discussed earlier, to the man who is standing to her left. The message is then passed around the coven in like manner. The last person to receive the message goes to the Priest who stands arms crossed in the west and whispers to him the message.

The Priest announces the intention of the rite:

> **It is to (intention),**
> **That is our intention here tonight.**

The coven ask the crone:

Give to us the true intention to bring our wish to birth.

The Priestess makes a supplication to the God of the Underworld for the safe passage of the coven and the absolution of their sins:

O Thou who art Lord of the Mound,
King of the Summerland,
Give to us the wisdom to walk freely
Upon our true path in this life.
Look upon our sacrifice with compassion
And absolve us from our sins.

The Priestess burns the offering and continues:

That we may we travel safely in the darkness,
Free from malice and evil thoughts.

The Priest then leads the coven in the dance of the Lame God - this is enacted to remind the coven of their imperfections (the Lame God is of Babylonian origin as are sin offerings). Dragging one leg behind him, the Priest begins the dance anticlockwise while they call the witch's rune. During the dance, each person in turn breaks away and goes to the High Priestess (who is the Dark Goddess) and whispers to her of their sins. They then light a small candle and give it to her as a gift and rejoin the dance. When the last person has given the Priestess their gift, the dance ends. The Priestess then takes up a candle and leads the coven thrice around the circle widdershins and leads the coven to the underworld.

When the slow procession has finished, the coven gathers around the Priest. The Priest asks if anyone wishes to make talismans or supplications to the Dark God for the gifts he bestows. Each person that requires something must write their wish upon a piece of paper in black ink. Those that wish to make talismans, do so. Near the end of the rite, the Priest stands in the west in the posture of Osiris slain (arms crossed) and the papers are collected in by the Priestess. The Priestess approaches the Priest, who impersonates the Dark God and gives him the petitions with the words:

Take our wish and give it birth,
Ye who dwell in darkest earth.
Time and tide will unite
To give it birth if it be right.
Hear our prayer, O dreadful God,
By the flame that is our rod.
Hear your children here below,
Grant our wish and mercy show.

The Priest then consecrates the talismans and burns the wishes. The Priestess leads the coven in a slow clockwise procession around the circle, leading them in the ascent to the land of the living. After the journey, the ceremony of cakes and wine is held and after a time, the circle closed.

THE RITE OF THE SUN

A pollo, the God of the Sun, is invoked for the purpose of obtaining good health, wealth, warmth, splendour and plenty. The sun shows itself outwardly and warmly, as do the Gods associated with the sun. All the Sun Gods are the enemies of evil and have the power to dispel darkness.

PREPARATION FOR THE RITE

For the Rite of the Sun, the circle should be cast at dawn or midday, preferably on Sunday, which is the time allotted to the Sun Gods. Any incense burned must be spicy, rich and warm (of a solar nature). The altar cloth, the candles and the robes must be gold or orange in colour. Gold is the metal of the sun and golden charms may be blessed at this time. The temple should be adorned with oak branches and acorns. For this rite you will need a solar wand, flowers for the maidens' hair, and a cauldron. Each person is given a taper before the rite and the cauldron placed in the centre of the circle.

THE RITE

The Priestess casts the circle in the usual manner and the circle is declared open. The Priest, who is standing in the sign of the Horned God (arms raised), begins the rite with an invocation to the God of the Sun:

> **The Rite of the Sun is about to start,**
> **Awake from sleep and takest heart.**
> **Gold and glory shall be thine**
> **Upon thee all his light shall shine.**

> Follow me in the spiral dance.
> Blessed be the Sun God's lance.
> As above, so below,
> Through the golden gate we go!

The Priest lights a candle and puts the candle in the cauldron, he then takes up the solar wand and raises it high above his head. The Priest begins to walk deosil around the circle and the Priestess takes the hand of another and follows him in the dance. The Priestess leads the coven in the spiral dance following the Priest who with every circuit moves closer to the centre. Once the Priest arrives at the centre of the circle, he lights the tapers from the cauldron. The coven gather around him and he (beginning with the Priestess) lights each person's taper with the charge:

> See how now the flame burns bright,
> See now how our hearts unite.
> Bright is the light from the sun
> Which makes us all become as one.
> Take this flame and may it be,
> Carried within eternally.

The Priestess places a flower in each woman's hair (the flower represents the bestowing of the gift of beauty). All this done, the Priest crosses to the altar and takes up the phallic wand. Raising the wand above his head, the Priest invokes the Sun God:

> As we gaze upon thy might,
> We call to thee, O Lord of Light,
> Bringer of life and fertility,
> Without whom we would not be.
> Let the path of the great sun wheel,
> Show us the path beneath our heel,
> Merrily we sing and prance
> As we dance the spiral dance.

The Priest then takes the hand of the Priestess and leads the coven in the spiral dance moving with the sun:

> Great is the sun; great is his might,
> Follow we shall into the light,
> Feel it within, feel it without,
> As joyously we sing and shout.

At a signal from the Priest, the dance stops and the coven gather around the cauldron. The Priest motions for the coven to sit and addresses the coven:

> **Gaze upon the flame and warm**
> **Yourselves in its heat.**
> **Not for nothing was the eternal**
> **Flame ever kept burning.**
> **And so it must always be so,**
> **For without it we shall perish.**

The Priest then asks if there is any magical working to be done that involves obtaining wealth, good health, or beauty. Charms and spells are then made and they are either burned or consecrated accordingly.

After a time the circle closed in the usual manner.

THE RITE OF VENUS

The planet Venus is visible in the night sky as a green light; this is why the Goddess Venus is associated with the colour green. The Goddess of Love is known by many names; Venus, Aphrodite, Ishtar, Isis, Freya, and many others. Although the names vary, the intention of the rite remains the same. Ritual supplications to the Goddess of Love and Compassion are often made to ask for her blessing in affairs of the heart. Only those whose hearts truly suffer can approach the Goddess of Compassion for understanding. For spells of love, sympathetic magic is often used to attract one person to another. If the aspects are good, the couple well suited, and the motive pure, love will eventually come if it is destined.

Sometimes love is confused with lust. Love and lust are different. Love is a great spiritual emotion, a longing for companionship. Lust is a lower bestial urge that dwells within us all for the reproduction of the species and it must be controlled.

The rites of Venus are performed at the discretion of the Priest and Priestess. Usually a member of the coven asks for this rite either for themselves or on the behalf of a friend. If a love ritual is to be performed for an outsider, then a love charm can be made and given to them later. If it is a matter of compassion, then a ritual supplication can be made on their behalf. If the despairing person is a member of the coven, the Priest and Priestess will make a supplication on their behalf or if it is a matter of love, attempt to find them a partner within the Craft.

PREPARATION FOR THE RITE

The Rite of Venus may be enacted upon the full or the waxing phase of the moon or upon the time and day allotted to the Goddess Venus. For the rite, the altar cloth, the candles and the robes should be a Venus green. Incense burned should be subtle and feminine and perfumes worn should be floral. Fresh blossoms and flowers must adorn the temple, especially roses. A bell is also required or a systrum.

THE RITE

The circle is cast in the traditional manner. To signal the beginning of the rite a bell is struck seven times or a systrum is shaken. The men form a circle around the cauldron and the women move to form a circle around the outside of the men. The Priestess then calls upon the Goddess of Love to descend to them:

> **Folkvang 'tis called where Freya may be,**
> **The loveliest Goddess in heaven is she.**
> **Vanadis on earth and Ishtar in heaven.**
> **Mother of the stars times seven.**
> **Listen to our hearts O Goddess above,**
> **And know of our secret yearning for love.**
> **Then whisper to us O eternal Goddess,**
> **With honeyed breath of soft caress,**
> **And tell us thy secrets of love without strife**
> **Hidden in thy beauty is a lust for life!**

The Priestess addresses the women of the coven:

> **Approach the man of thy choice,**
> **And grant him the token of thy lips.**

The women step towards a man of their choosing and kiss him. Each pair in turn join hands and raise them above their heads to show that they are joined. The coven begins to walk clockwise around the circle. As each couple pass the Priest and Priestess, they raise their hands to show their bonding.

The Priestess calls:

> **And they shall be naked in their rite!**

The coven removes their attire and the Priest then draws down the Goddess into the body of the Priestess with the five-fold salute (see drawing down the moon).

> Come to us O Goddess in thy wondrous form,
> And let us glimpse once more
> The passion in your eyes,
> Let us gaze upon your beauty,
> O consort of the Gods.
> Naked in thy splendour,
> Lady of the evening star
> Smile on us, and your blessings give,
> So that we may love once more!

The Priestess then invokes the God down into the body of the Priest. The Priestess adopts the posture of Mater Triumphant (covering her breasts with her right hand and her groin with her left hand) and addresses the Priest:

> I am the Goddess Aphrodite,
> Hand me my instrument,
> That I may stir the winds of desire
> That cause the breath to quicken.

The Priestess is handed a tambourine by the Priest with a kiss. Moving in a slow sensual dance around the circle, the Priestess shakes the tambourine. In some covens, the men and the women who have been paired together, brush against each other as they pass (if they wish to). This generates an enormous amount of sexual energy with which to charge the love charms. After the dance has ended, the Priest proclaims:

> The rite is done - The Goddess is among us!

LOVE CHARMS FOR ATTRACTING A LOVER

Love charms can be constructed for this purpose made from copper, the metal sacred to the Goddess of Love, or from paper and green ink. These charms may bear the name of the desired, or their magical number. A personal belonging of the loved one can also be charged and carried upon the person to draw them near to you. The charms are then to be consecrated and charged in the manner prescribed.

CANDLE SPELL FOR ATTRACTING A LOVER.

For this rite, the following items are required: some red thread, an extra green candle (for her) and a red candle (for him). The candles are to be anointed with scented oil. The candles are then tied together with the red thread. The thread is to be wound around the green candle for a man who is attracting a woman, and wound around the red candle for a woman who is attracting a man. The Priestess writes upon the green candle the name of the woman and on the red candle the name of the man. The candles are to be charged with the invocation:

> **Upon this candle I shall write,**
> **What I require of thee tonight.**

The words "Come see" are to be written upon the candle of the desirer. The Priestess lights the candles:

> **Fire glow, vision show**
> **Of the heart's desire,**
> **When the spell is chanted**
> **Of the witches' fire.**
> **Red string, love to bring**
> **When the candles turning,**
> **Chant the spell and be it done**
> **While the fire's burning!**

As the candles burn lower, wind the thread around the candle of the desirer, thus bringing the desired closer as the thread shortens.

The circle is eventually closed in the prescribed manner and the candles are left to burn down safely overnight. The couples then leave together to conclude their own rituals.

THE RITE OF JUPITER

The planet Jupiter is a large planet that can be seen to the human eye as a blue light in the night sky. Jupiter is hailed as the greatest of the Gods and he presides over all others. He is a God of joy, luck, magnanimity, and honour.

PREPARATION FOR THE RITE

The circle should be cast during the time of the full or waxing moon, or upon the times allotted to them. The altar cloth, the candles, and the ceremonial attire should be blue (candles need to be sufficient in quantity to give adequate light). An incense blend containing Cedarwood is suitable. Cedarwood is one of the trees sacred to the Great Gods and it was used by the Egyptians and the Babylonians for incense. Oak or chestnut, blossom or fruit may be used to adorn the temple. The horse chestnut has connections with the Great Gods through Poseidon who loved to race white horses. For this rite a horseshoe and a cup of mead is required, but it is not essential. The coven must assemble in a joyful, hopeful manner. This is essential to the working.

THE RITE

The circle is cast in the usual manner, and the Priestess takes up the cup of mead (this can be wine). The Priestess raises her cup in salute to the Great Gods and makes the invocation to Jupiter:

> **I raise my cup in salute to Jupiter,**
> **The greatest of all the Gods!**
> **Great is Jupiter, and I pray that he will**

Come amongst us and grant us all good fortune.
I dedicate this mead* to the Greatest of the Gods.
And in the drinking thereof, may we also achieve greatness.

*The Greek Gods were believed to only drink Ambrosia, a honey-wine
similar to mead.

The Priestess then drinks from the cup and passes the cup to the
Priest with a kiss and the usual blessing:

From me to thee, blessed be.

The Priest accepts the cup and returns the blessing. He drinks from
the cup also, and the cup is then passed to the coven for them to drink
from:

Partake ye of the good fortune of Jupiter,
And know ye this, if there be work to be done,
Enjoy it, happiness will be thrice rewarded,
Be at peace and enjoy the gifts that Jupiter bestows.

After the last person has partaken of the mead, the Priestess calls:

O ye of the joyous craft, come join me in the dance!

A lively dance around the circle then ensues to a merry tune. After
the dance, the Priestess proclaims aloud:

Now does great Jupiter dwell among us,
Let us give him homage.

At this point in the rite, the Priestess calls:

Where is he that represents the God?

A member of the coven then steps forward to impersonate the God
Jupiter. The Priestess crowns him with a wreath of Oak or Chestnut
leaves. The coven kneels and they all bow to him. The coven greet
him saying:

Hail Jupiter! We greet thee,
Welcome art thou.

The coven all rise and the Priestess leads the dance, skipping around the circle. After the dance, the Priestess raises up the horseshoe and calls upon Jupiter:

> **Great is the God of pale blue sky,**
> **Pray, grant our wishes by and by,**
> **Let thy blessings upon us shine**
> **By horseshoe, pin and finger sign,**
> **Four-leaf clover we shall show**
> **To bring us luck wherever we go,**
> **Which way to go? Thou must know,**
> **Help us, guide us, good luck flow.**

Any good luck charms can then be made. Tin is the metal assigned to this God, but it is hard to work, so it is better to write spells on paper, in blue ink, or to obtain a lucky charm that can be consecrated and charged. After a time the circle is closed in the usual manner.

APPENDIX A
THE TABLE OF CORRESPONDENCES

JUPITER

Colour:	Purple, azure blue.
Metal:	Tin.
Gemstones:	Amethyst, sapphire.
Tarot card:	The Hierophant.
Plants:	Hyssop, saffron.
Trees:	Cedar, lilac.
Perfumes:	Woody smells.
Animals:	Eagle, unicorn.
Other names:	Zeus, Anu, Odin.
Chakra:	The crown.
Weapon:	The sceptre or wand.
Physical:	Liver and hormones.
Day:	Thursday.
Hour:	See table of hours.
Figure:	Square.
Number:	Four.
Zodiac signs:	Capricorn, Pisces,Cancer.
Incense:	Copal gum.
Oil:	Cedarwood.
Angel:	Sachiel.
Aspects:	Luck, success.
Sephira:	Chesed.

 MERCURY

Colours:	Black & white, rainbow.
Metal:	Mercury, all alloys.
Gemstones:	Opal, agate, alexandrine.
Tarot card:	I. The Magician.
Plants:	Fennel, dill, myrtle.
Trees:	Hazel.
Perfumes:	Lemon, citrus, lavender.
Animals:	Magpie, ibis, ape.
Names:	Hermes, Thoth.
Chakra:	Throat.
Weapon:	The caduceus.

Physical:	The oral system.
Day:	Wednesday.
Hour:	See table of hours.
Figure:	Octagram, octagon.
Number:	Eight.
Zodiac signs:	Gemini, Aquarius.
Incense:	Styrax gum.
Angel:	Raphael.
Aspects:	Eloquence, medicine.
Sephira:	Hod.

 SATURN

Colour:	Black.
Metal:	Lead.
Gemstones:	Onyx, obsidian, jet.
Tarot card:	The world.
Plants:	Nightshade, pansy.
Trees:	Black cypress, yew.
Perfumes:	Myrrh, civet, musk.
Animals:	Raven, crow, crocodile.
Names:	Kronos, Nudd, Osiris, Nergal.
Chakra:	Lignum anus.
Weapon:	Hourglass, scythe.
Physical:	Teeth, bones, spleen, genitals, skin.
Day:	Saturday.
Hour:	See table.
Figure:	Triangle.
Number:	Three.
Zodiac signs:	Virgo.
Incense:	Asafetida gum.
Oil:	Musks.
Angel:	Cassiel.
Aspect:	Dark, solemn, knowledgeable, literate.
Powers:	Death, change, karma.
Sephira:	Chokmah.

MOON

Colours:	Silver, white.
Metal:	Silver.
Gemstones:	Pearl, quartz, moonstone.
Tarot card:	The moon.

Plants:	Lotus, jasmine.
Trees:	Willow, eucalyptus.
Perfumes:	Clean, cool smells.
Animals:	Dog, owl, deer, hare.
Names:	Diana, Astarte, Aradia, Isis.
Chakra:	Third eye — Ajna
Weapon:	Bow and arrow.
Physical:	White fluids, lymph gland, stomach.
Day:	Monday.
Hour:	See table.
Figure:	Silver crescent.
Number:	Two.
Zodiac signs:	Cancer, Pisces.
Incense:	Damar gum.
Oil:	Ylang ylang.
Angel:	Gabriel.
Aspects:	Protective, enchanting, flowing, wise.
Powers:	Magic, ESP.
Sephira:	Yesod.

♂ MARS

Colour:	Red.
Metal:	Iron.
Gemstones:	Garnet, ruby.
Tarot card:	The emperor & the tower.
Plants:	Nettle, mustard, tobacco.
Trees:	Pine.
Perfumes:	Hot peppery smells.
Animals:	Basilisk, ram, wolf, bear.
Other names:	Aries, Tiu, Set, Nergal.
Chakra:	The heart.
Weapon:	The sword, scourge.
Physical:	Muscles, gonads, blood.
Day:	Tuesday.
Hour:	See table.
Figure:	Pentagram.
Number:	Five.
Zodiac signs:	Aries, Sagittarius.
Incense:	Opoponax gum.
Oil:	Ginger, galangal, pepper.
Angel:	Samael.
Aspect:	Hot, warlike, energetic.

Sigil:	Circle with an arrow.
Powers:	Courage, strength, masculinity, victory.
Sephira:	Geburah.

 SUN

Colour:	Yellow, gold, orange.
Metal:	Gold.
Gemstones:	Diamond, tiger's eye.
Tarot card:	The sun.
Plants:	Bay, heliotrope, saffron.
Trees:	Oak, bay.
Perfumes:	Spice, cinnamon, orange.
Animals:	Phoenix, lion.
Names:	Horus, Apollo, Nuada, Balder, Samas.
Chakra:	Solar plexus.
Weapon:	Breast plate.
Physical:	Heart, circulation,thymus
Day:	Sunday.
Hour:	See table.
Figure:	Circle with a dot inside.
Number:	One.
Zodiac signs:	Leo.
Incense:	Olibanum.
Oil:	Orange, cinnamon.
Angel:	Michael.
Aspect:	Warm, radiant.
Powers:	Wealth, health, splendour.
Sephira:	Tiphareth.

 VENUS

Colour:	Green.
Metal:	Copper.
Gemstones:	Emerald, jade.
Plants:	Vervain, rose, mint.
Trees:	Hawthorn.
Perfumes:	Rose, flowery scents.
Animals:	Dove, lynx.
Names:	Aphrodite, Freya, Ishtar.
Weapon:	Lamp, girdle.
Physical:	Menstruation, womb, kidneys, throat.
Day:	Friday.

Figure:	Heptagram.
Hour:	See table.
Zodiac signs:	Libra, Taurus.
Incense:	Elemi gum.
Tarot card:	III. The Empress.
Chakra:	Navel or spleen.
Number:	Seven.
Oils:	Mints and floral.
Aspect:	Compassionate, serene.
Sigil:	Circle over a cross.
Angel:	Anael.
Archangel:	Tarshishim.
Powers:	Love, mercy, beauty.
Sephira:	Netzach.

ELEMENTAL AIR

Tarot card:	Swords.
Colour:	Yellow.
Cardinal:	East.
Stone:	Chalcedony.
Archangel:	Raphael.
Angel:	Chassan.
Elemental:	Sylphs, valkyries.
Incense:	Galbanum.
God forms:	Ameshet, Nut, Anu.
Ruler:	Ariel.
Call:	Exarp.
King:	Paralda.
Weapon:	Fan.
Tattvic:	The yellow cube.

ELEMENTAL FIRE

Tarot card:	Wands.
Colour:	Red.
Cardinal:	South.
Stone:	Fire gems.
Archangel:	Michael.
Angel:	Aral.
Elemental:	Salamander, fire giants.
Incense:	Opoponax.
God forms:	Hades, Hel, Girru.

Ruler:	Djinn.
Call:	Bitom.
Weapon:	Triangle of fire.
Sigil:	Upright triangle.
Tattvic:	Red triangle.

 ## ELEMENTAL WATER

Tarot card:	Cups.
Colour:	Sea green.
Cardinal:	West.
Stone:	Aquamarine.
Archangel:	Gabriel.
Angel:	Taliahad.
Elemental:	Undine, mermaid.
Incense:	Labdanum.
God forms:	Neptune, Ea, Tefnut.
Ruler:	Tharsis.
Call:	Hcoma.
King:	Nichsa.
Sigil:	Inverted triangle.
Weapon:	Cross.
Tattvic:	Blue circle.

 ## ELEMENTAL EARTH

Tarot card:	Pentacles.
Colour:	Brown.
Cardinal:	North.
Stone:	Antimony.
Archangel:	Uriel.
Angel:	Phorlakh.
Elemental:	Gnomes.
Incense:	Styrax.
God forms:	Demeter, Geb, Bel.
Ruler:	Cherub.
Call:	Manta.
King:	Ghob.
Weapon:	Pentacle, salt.
Sigil:	Inverted triangle with a horizontal bar.

APPENDIX B
INCENSE FOR WICCA

Smells are extremely important in aiding visualisation as they create a mental impression on the subconscious. In the table of correspondences there is a list of planetary Gods and Goddesses and under their names are given the corresponding oils and incenses. If you are able to obtain the ingredients, you may make your own incense as did the witches of old. If you prefer to buy ready-made incense, you must trust that it has been suitably prepared.

Blends of essential oils can be burned in a scent censer as an alternative if you can't stand incense smoke, but make sure that the oils you are burning are not synthetic oils - as they smell like burning plastic!

INCENSE FOR SABBATS

IMBOLC
Blend together: 1 spoonful of thyme, 1 spoonful of cinnamon and 1 spoonful of fennel seed, add 1 spoonful of cypress leaves and 2 spoonfuls of pine gum to recreate the smell of pine woods.

BELTANE
Blend together: 1 spoonful of red sandalwood, 1 spoonful of rose petals, 1 spoonful of cinnamon, 1 spoonful of cedarwood and 2 spoonfuls of labdanum or myrrh gum. It's cheaper to use myrrh gum and add a couple of drops of labdanum oil to give this incense a smell like that of smoke and sap.

OSTARA
Mix together: 1 spoonful of fennel seed and 1 spoonful of juniper berry, 1 spoonful of sandalwood. 1 spoonful of rose petals and 2 spoonfuls of elemi gum, for a rich, light, spring smell.

LITHA
Blend together: 2 spoonfuls of copal gum, 1 spoonful of lemon verbena, 1 spoonful of rose petals, 1 spoonful of mint, and 1 spoonful of cinnamon. Add a few drops of almond oil, to create a flowery midsummer smell.

MABON
Mix together: 1 spoonful of calamus root, 1 spoonful of cinnamon and 1 spoonful of juniper berry, 1 spoonful of nutmeg, and 2 spoonfuls of copal gum for that dry, autumn smell.

SAMHAIN
Blend together: 2 spoonfuls of opoponax gum, 1 spoonful of cypress, 1 spoonful of rue, 1 spoonful of angelica root, and 1

spoonful of fennel seed. A musk oil suitable for burning can also be added to heighten the musky Halloween smell.

LAMMAS
For a Lammas incense, mix 2 spoonfuls of copal gum, 1 spoonful of meadowsweet and 1 spoonful of chamomile flowers. 1 spoonful of golden rod and 1 spoonful of rose petals.

YULE
For a spicy Yule smell, mix 1 spoonful of pine gum, 1 spoon of copal gum and 1 spoon of frankincense gum, add 1 spoonful of mistletoe herb and 1 spoonful of juniper berry, add 1 spoonful of aniseed and 1 spoonful of herb of basil.

ESBAT
For an incense to burn at the full moon meetings, mix together: 1 spoonful of myrrh and 1 spoonful of frankincense gum, 1 spoonful of sandalwood and 1 spoonful of orris root, 1 spoonful of lemon verbena and 1 spoonful of rose petals. Add a few drops of ylang ylang or rose oil if desired.

INCENSE FOR PLANETARY RITES

SATURN INCENSE
For a dark Saturnine incense, mix together: 1 spoonful of asafetida gum, 1 spoonful of myrrh gum, 1 spoonful of bay leaves and 1 spoonful of cypress, 1 spoonful of rue and 1 spoonful of angelica root, add a few drops of a musk oil..

JUPITER INCENSE
Mix together: 2 spoonfuls of copal gum, 1 spoonful of sandalwood and 1 spoonful of cedarwood, 1 spoonful of cinnamon, 1 spoonful of juniper berry, add a few drops of cedarwood oil.

MARS INCENSE
Blend together: 2 spoonfuls of opoponax gum, 1 spoonful of dark tobacco, 1 spoonful of poppy flowers, 1 spoonful of sichuan peppers or basil and 1 spoonful of coriander seed.

SOLAR INCENSE
For a good solar incense, mix together: 1 spoonful of elemi gum and 1 spoonful of myrrh gum, 1 spoonful of orange peel and 1 spoonful of clove buds, 1 spoonful of cinnamon, and 1 spoonful of nutmeg, add a few drops of caramel, orange, or bay oil to get a rich smell.

VENUS INCENSE
Mix together: 1 spoonful of pine gum and 1 spoonful of benzoin gum, 1 spoonful of thyme and 1 spoonful of rose petals, 1 spoonful

of mint, and 1 spoonful of calamus root, add a few drops of rose oil for a rich flowery scent.

MERCURY INCENSE
Blend 1 spoonful of elemi gum, 1 spoonful of frankincense, 1 spoonful of orange peel, 1 spoonful of bay, 1 spoonful of lemon verbena, and 1 spoonful of dill seed, 1 spoonful of lavender for a light, but slightly sharp smell.

LUNAR INCENSE
Mix together: 2 spoonfuls of damar gum, 1 spoonful of rosemary and 1 spoonful of rose petals, 1 spoonful of lemon verbena and 1 spoonful of lavender, add a few drops of camphorated oil for a cool, clean smell.

ELEMENTAL INCENSES

EARTH INCENSE
Blend together: 1 spoonful of pine resin, 1 spoonful of myrrh gum, 1 spoonful of bay leaves and 1 spoonful of thyme, 1 spoonful of cypress and 1 spoonful of costus beans, add a few drops of patchouli oil for an earthy smell.

SPIRIT INCENSE
Mix together: 1 spoonful of benzoin, 1 spoonful of styrax gum, 1 spoonful of cinnamon, 1 spoonful of aniseed, 1 spoonful of juniper berry and 1 spoonful of rose petals, add a few drops of amber oil for a rich, dark warm smell.

AIR INCENSE
Blend: 1 spoonful of mastic gum, 1 spoonful of damar gum, and 1 spoonful of frankincense gum. 1 spoonful of bay leaves, 1 spoonful of rosemary and 1 spoonful of lavender for a light airy smell.

FIRE INCENSE
Mix together: 1 spoonful of opoponax gum, 1 spoonful of benzoin, and 1 spoonful of chinese aniseed and 1 spoonful of rose petals, 1 spoonful of sichuan peppers or ginger, and 1 spoonful of basil, for a warm, dark, fiery scent.

WATER INCENSE
Mix together: 2 spoonfuls of rose petals, 1 spoonful of benzoin gum, 1 spoonful of styrax, 1 spoonful of allspice, 1 spoonful of cinnamon, add a few drops of jasmine or labdanum can also be added to this blend.

TABLES OF PLANETARY HOURS

Sunday

1st	2nd	3rd	4th	5th	6th	7th	8th	9th	10th	11th	12th
Sun	Moon	Mars	Merc	Jupi	Venu	Satu	Sun	Moon	Mars	Merc	Jupi

13th	14th	15th	16th	17th	18th	19th	20th	21st	22nd	23rd	24th
Venu	Satu	Sun	Moon	Mars	Merc	Jupi	Venu	Satu	Sun	Moon	Mars

Monday

1st	2nd	3rd	4th	5th	6th	7th	8th	9th	10th	11th	12th
Moon	Mars	Merc	Jupi	Venu	Satu	Sun	Moon	Mars	Merc	Jupi	Venu

13th	14th	15th	16th	17th	18th	19th	20th	21st	22nd	23rd	24th
Satu	Sun	Moon	Mars	Merc	Jupi	Venu	Satu	Sun	Moon	Mars	Merc

Tuesday

1st	2nd	3rd	4th	5th	6th	7th	8th	9th	10th	11th	12th
Mars	Merc	Jupi	Venu	Satu	Sun	Moon	Mars	Merc	Jupi	Venu	Satu

13th	14th	15th	16th	17th	18th	19th	20th	21st	22nd	23rd	24th
Sun	Moon	Mars	Merc	Jupi	Venu	Satu	Sun	Moon	Mars	Merc	Jupi

Wednesday

1st	2nd	3rd	4th	5th	6th	7th	8th	9th	10th	11th	12th
Merc	Jupi	Venu	Satu	Sun	Moon	Mars	Merc	Jupi	Venu	Satu	Sun

13th	14th	15th	16th	17th	18th	19th	20th	21st	22nd	23rd	24th
Moon	Mars	Merc	Jupi	Venu	Satu	Sun	Moon	Mars	Merc	Jupi	Venu

Thursday

1st	2nd	3rd	4th	5th	6th	7th	8th	9th	10th	11th	12th
Jupi	Venu	Satu	Sun	Moon	Mars	Merc	Jupi	Venu	Satu	Sun	Moon

13th	14th	15th	16th	17th	18th	19th	20th	21st	22nd	23rd	24th
Mars	Merc	Jupi	Venu	Satu	Sun	Moon	Mars	Merc	Jupi	Venu	Satu

Friday

1st	2nd	3rd	4th	5th	6th	7th	8th	9th	10th	11th	12th
Venu	Satu	Sun	Moon	Mars	Merc	Jupi	Venu	Satu	Sun	Moon	Mars

13th	14th	15th	16th	17th	18th	19th	20th	21st	22nd	23rd	24th
Merc	Jupi	Venu	Satu	Sun	Moon	Mars	Merc	Jupi	Venu	Satu	Sun

Saturday

1st	2nd	3rd	4th	5th	6th	7th	8th	9th	10th	11th	12th
Satu	Sun	Moon	Mars	Merc	Jupi	Venu	Satu	Sun	Moon	Mars	Merc

13th	14th	15th	16th	17th	18th	19th	20th	21st	22nd	23rd	24th
Jupi	Venu	Satu	Sun	Moon	Mars	Merc	Jupi	Venu	Satu	Sun	Moon

OTHER SUGGESTED READING

There are also many other books about Wicca and Wiccan related subjects that are worth while reading, they are as follows:

JANET & STUART FARRAR	*WHAT WITCHES DO* *THE LIFE AND TIMES OF A MODERN WITCH* *THE WITCHES GOD* *THE WITCHES GODDESS* *THE WITCHES WAY* *THE EIGHT SABBATS FOR WITCHES*
GERALD GARDNER	*WITCHCRAFT FOR TODAY* *THE MEANING OF WITCHCRAFT*
ROBERT GRAVES	*THE WHITE GODDESS.*
PATRICIA CROWTHER	*LID OFF THE CAULDRON*
CHARLES LELAND	*ARADIA: THE GOSPEL OF THE WITCHES*
DOREEN VALIENTE	*WITCHCRAFT- A TRADITION RENEWED* *ABC OF WITCHCRAFT* *NATURAL MAGIC*
DeLAWRENCE	*THE BOOK OF ABRA-MELIN THE MAGE,* *THE GOETIA* *THE KEY OF SOLOMON* *THE KEY TO THE TAROT*
ALEISTER CROWLEY	*777* *THE RITES OF ELEUSIS*
SIR J.G. FRAZER	*THE GOLDEN BOUGH*